Entrepreneurship and how to establish your own business

Seventh edition

Tersia Botha (Editor)

juta

Entrepreneurship and how to establish your own business

First published 1996
Second edition 2001
Third edition 2007
Fourth edition 2012
Fifth edition 2015
Sixth edition 2018
Seventh edition 2022

Juta and Company (Pty) Ltd
First floor, Sunclare building, 21 Dreyer Street, Claremont 7708
PO Box 14373, Lansdowne 7779, Cape Town, South Africa
www.juta.co.za

ISBN 978 1 48513 258 5 (Print)
ISBN 978 1 48513 259 2 (WebPDF)

Project Specialist: Fuzlin Toffar
Editor: Rod Prodgers
Proofreader: Lee-Ann Ashcroft
Cover designer: Renaissance Studio
Typesetter: LT Design Worx
Indexer: Lexinfo

Acknowledgement:
Table 1.1 – Reproduced under Government Printers Authorisation (Authorisation no.11800) dated 13 November 2018

Typeset in 10 pt on 13 pt Meridien LT Std

Contents

Preface

The transformation of ideas into economic opportunities is the crux of entrepreneurship. History shows that pragmatic people who are entrepreneurial, creative and innovative, able to exploit opportunities and willing to take risks have significantly advanced economic progress. For example, the USA gets more than half of its economic growth from industries that barely existed a decade ago. This is directly attributable to innovative entrepreneurs and their start-up businesses.

Entrepreneurs can produce new solutions to old problems, and they always challenge the status quo. Entrepreneurs are risk-takers who pursue opportunities that others may fail to recognise or may even view as problems or threats. Entrepreneurs are closely associated with change, creativity, knowledge, innovation and flexibility, which are all factors that are increasingly important sources of competitiveness in an increasingly globalised world economy. Therefore, fostering entrepreneurship means promoting the competitiveness of businesses.

At a macro-level private sector development and entrepreneurship development are essential ingredients for achieving the United Nations Millennium Development Goal of reducing poverty. While sound macroeconomic policies and providing market access are crucial, emerging markets need to nurture and develop entrepreneurs able to take advantage of the opportunities created by globalisation.

At a national level, entrepreneurs can play a vital role in the economic development of the country and the social upliftment of its people. As with the rest of the private sector, entrepreneurial development is a powerful engine of economic growth and wealth creation, and crucial for improving the quality, number and variety of employment opportunities for the poor. Economically, entrepreneurship invigorates markets. The formation of new business leads to job creation and has a multiplying effect on the economy. Socially, entrepreneurship empowers citizens, generates innovation and changes mindsets. These changes have the potential to integrate developing countries successfully into the global economy.

The aim of this book is to introduce the reader to entrepreneurship and to guide him/her through the establishment of his/her own business, from the identification and development of the business idea, through the feasibility and viability studies, the crafting of a well-structured business plan, the financing and implementation of the business plan, to the start and management of the business. In terms of setting up a business, the various business forms (ie sole proprietorship, partnership, private company, close corporation) and business function (ie marketing, public relations, information and record keeping, finance, human resources, purchasing, operations, and general management) are also addressed.

The authors welcome you to *Entrepreneurship and how to establish your own business.*

Prof Tersia Botha
April 2022

About the authors

Prof Tersia Botha from the Department of Business Management at the University of South Africa (Unisa), holds a DCom degree in finance and investment management and has been lecturing for more than 30 years. She has published research articles in the fields of general management, finance and investment management and contributed to numerous books on finance, business management, general management, corporate citizenship, leadership, global business management, business management by portfolio, strategy and responsible management.

Prof Alex Antonites is the head of the Department of Business Management, University of Pretoria (UP). He is also an MBA lecturer at the Gordon Institute of Business Sciences (GIBS) and head of the UP-Business Incubator. He specialises in the field of entrepreneurship and small business development with a specific focus on the pre-entrepreneurial phase concerning creativity, innovation and opportunity finding.

Prof Michael Cant is a professor in the Department of Marketing and Retail at the University of South Africa (Unisa).

Mr Andreas de Beer is a senior lecturer in the Department of Business Management at the University of South Africa (Unisa).

Dr Hannelize Jacobs is a co-founder and director at LEAP Academy for Graduates and Professionals and formerly an associate professor in Management at Monash University. In her academic career of more than 25 years, she has served in various managerial and leadership positions in South Africa and abroad. She has published widely and presented her research all over the world. Her research focuses predominantly on entrepreneurial and innovative behaviour, and how to strategically manage and lead for innovation.

Prof Cecile Nieuwenhuizen is professor and chair of the DHET-NRF SARChI Entrepreneurship Education at the University of Johannesburg (UJ). She is also involved in various entrepreneurial family businesses. Her field of specialisation includes entrepreneurship, innovation, management and leadership.

Ms Adele van Lille is a lecturer in the Department of Business Management at the University of South Africa (Unisa).

ENTREPRENEURSHIP AND SMALL, MEDIUM AND MICRO ENTERPRISES IN PERSPECTIVE

CECILE NIEUWENHUIZEN

LEARNING OUTCOMES

After you have studied this chapter, you should be able to:

- LO 1: Define the terms 'entrepreneur' and 'entrepreneurship'
- LO 2: Indicate the relationship between entrepreneurship, a small business enterprise and small business management
- LO 3: Explain the various types of entrepreneurial businesses
- LO 4: Explain corporate entrepreneurship/intrapreneurship
- LO 5: Explain the key success factors of entrepreneurs
- LO 6: Explain how entrepreneurs should deal with external factors that affect their businesses

Introduction

Employment opportunities abound in private and public sector organisations. Schools, colleges and universities primarily teach and train us to become employees, not employers. However, those of us who identify and evaluate the best employers often agree that our best employers are ourselves. This is measured by work satisfaction, experience, income, self-realisation, job creation and a range of other factors.

Unfortunately, we are often incorrectly informed that entrepreneurship cannot be learnt, that entrepreneurship is an innate ability and few are born with it. Fortunately, this is untrue: it has been proved that entrepreneurship is a discipline, and therefore can be taught and learnt through specialised entreprencurship education (Kuratko, 2014). Although entrepreneurship is a relatively new discipline, research and education in entrepreneurship have increased tremendously in recent decades. It is now known what entrepreneurship is and how it should be taught. It is crucial that entrepreneurship programmes should not be short, superficial courses but possess depth. In addition, entrepreneurship education is notably different from business or business management education; lecturers have to learn how to teach true entrepreneurship that makes a difference to the lives of entrepreneurs, their communities and the economy.

Furthermore, entrepreneurial activity has a crucial influence on the national economy: more than a source of income, it is a stimulant – a source of innovation. In fact, economic development can be directly attributed to levels of entrepreneurial activity in a national economy. In high-growth, globally competitive economies the ability to nurture entrepreneurial activity, grow businesses, create wealth and sustain competitive advantage is imperative. There is a direct correlation between job creation and the level of entrepreneurial activity in an economy, and a statistically significant association between national economic growth and entrepreneurship (Kuratko, 2014:xxxii). Entrepreneurial businesses ensure economic growth by means of innovation, which creates wealth for the entrepreneur and adds value to society.

This introductory chapter explains how the entrepreneur and entrepreneurship relate to a small business and small business management. Subsequently the different types of entrepreneurial businesses as well as corporate entrepreneurship are introduced. The key success factors that contribute to successful entrepreneurship are explained, and information on the external factors affecting entrepreneurship are provided.

LO 1: Define the terms 'entrepreneur' and 'entrepreneurship'

1.1   Defining entrepreneur and entrepreneurship

DEFINITION   Entrepreneurs have the ability to identify and seize an opportunity and create and develop a business by adding value to the business. They do this by applying resources that include finance, time, effort, people and skills. They are willing to take risks; and through their businesses they organise, manage and achieve results.

EXAMPLE 1.1

Entrepreneurs can therefore be described as those people who:

- start their own business
- manage the business
- identify new products or opportunities
- seize opportunities
- create and innovate
- organise and control resources of capital, labour and materials to realise profit

- have the ability and insight to market, produce and finance a service or product
- have the financial means, or access to finance, to realise the business
- are willing to take calculated risks.

Entrepreneurship is the process of establishing a business, from the identification of a business opportunity and innovation through to planning, start-up, managing and growing the business. Entrepreneurship is, therefore, also acknowledged as a discipline on its own.

It is important to keep in mind that not everyone who starts a new business is actually an entrepreneur. Some might be *enterprising*, but a true entrepreneur habitually creates and *innovates* to build and develop something of recognisable value. Not all small, medium and micro enterprises (SMMEs) achieve something new or different, nor do all grow and become successful. Thus, although small businesses create wealth and add value to the economy, not all SMMEs are *entrepreneurial*.

SMMEs, not necessarily entrepreneurial businesses, form around 90% of all registered businesses in South Africa. Their contribution to the country's gross domestic product (GDP) is 36% and they provide employment to 60% of the workforce. In the USA, United Kingdom, Germany, France and other developed countries, small businesses contribute more than 50% to the GDP of each country (GEM, 2018). Due to the Covid-19 pandemic there was a decrease in entrepreneurial activity in the majority of countries between 2019 and 2020. In some countries entrepreneurial activity fell by more than 25%, whereas entrepreneurial activity increased in a minority of countries (GEM, 2021). This had a significant impact on the provision of employment by SMMEs in the world economy.

DEFINITION	Gross domestic product (GDP) is the total production of a country.
	The total number of services and products supplied and produced within the borders of a country in one year is measured in financial terms by GDP. The growth rate of GDP is an indication of how successful a country is in providing jobs and income to its citizens.

LO 2: Indicate the relationship between entrepreneurship, a small business enterprise and small business management

1.2 The relationship between entrepreneurship, a small business enterprise and small business management

Most businesses begin as small or micro enterprises, usually managed by a single person. That person's aim is to grow and develop the business. This can happen continuously as long as the entrepreneur retains their entrepreneurial mindset (ie continues to innovate and create). However, if the entrepreneur becomes comfortable and satisfied with the level of growth of the enterprise, they stop being an entrepreneur and become a small business manager, who is risk-, change- and innovation-averse. Schumpeter (1934) observes that most businesses settle for non-entrepreneurial stability; Katz and Green (2014:9) confirm this, suggesting that those that do are usually lifestyle or part-time businesses that start and remain small, and contribute to living costs. They represent approximately 53% of small businesses. According to them, traditional small businesses are very small, operate from a single site and have reached a sufficient level of income: at most, their growth will be inflation related.

EXAMPLE 1.2

Examples of a small business manager who is not an entrepreneur are:

- a person who manages an existing business or franchise such as a Trellidor[1] franchise without ensuring growth

- a person who works full- or part-time in a lifestyle business, such as a bed and breakfast guesthouse that does not generate sufficient income to cover all living expenses

- a person satisfied with a no-growth, 'single-premise' business, for example a boutique in a shopping mall

- a person who inherits a business and runs it in the same way as their predecessor, for example a child who inherits a parent's farm and continues farming without expanding or improving it

- a person appointed by the owner of a small business as the manager.

Successful entrepreneurs and small business owners should also be able to manage a business that is in the process of growing and has grown. The danger is that when the business has grown to a certain size, the entrepreneur may lack the skills to manage the business even though they may be competent and innovative. An extreme example: in 2007 the successful entrepreneur, Hamdi Ulukaya, started his own business, Chobani Inc, selling Greek yoghurt. By 2015, it had achieved $1 billion in annual sales. But the growth of the business exceeded his ability to manage it, leading to problems that included financial losses, high debt, scattered operations, a lack of purchasing power and inadequate quality control. Mr Ulukaya came to realise that he had to appoint a chief executive officer with management expertise (Gasparro, 2015:10). Many successful entrepreneurs are able to establish and grow their businesses, but are not as competent in managing medium or large businesses. It is essential that the entrepreneur acknowledge this and ensure that a competent business manager is appointed.

---

1. A manufacturer and installer of home and business security, the business was established in Durban in the 1980s. It has managed successful growth by franchising its operations and now has about 69 outlets nationally and 17 in other countries, including 11 in Africa.

A small business manager must therefore be able to:
- plan, organise, lead and control the various business functions
- organise the efficient performance of tasks
- ensure interpersonal and inter-group competence
- facilitate formal communication during scheduled meetings
- compile and implement necessary policies and procedures for the business.

LO 3: Explain the various types of entrepreneurial businesses

Successful entrepreneurs are not always successful managers. In fast growth phases this can become a threat to the business. Entrepreneurs should acknowledge their strengths and weaknesses, such as limitations on time, attention and energy. The entrepreneur may have to upgrade their management skills; hire a professional manager; or both. Employees should be managed.

1.3   Types of entrepreneurial businesses

Entrepreneurial businesses can be classified as either informal, micro, very small, small, medium or large. Each type of business has very specific characteristics with specific needs and features. Some of these are discussed in the section below.

The National Small Enterprise Act 102 of 1996 as amended by the National Small Business Amendment Act 26 of 2003 and the National Small Enterprise Amendment Bill of 2020 have set out criteria defining business size in each sector of industry (see Table 1.1).

1.3.1   The formal small business

Formal businesses are all micro, small, medium and large businesses that are registered and compliant to legislation and regulations affecting businesses such as tax, labour, black economic empowerment and other laws and regulations.

The small and micro business sector

In the National Small Enterprise Act 102 of 1996 as amended by the National Small Business Amendment Act 26 of 2003 and the National Small Enterprise Amendment Bill of 2020, a micro business is defined as a business with five or fewer employees with a turnover of up to R100 000 per annum. A very small business employs between one and ten employees, and a small business between 11 and 50 employees. The upper limit for annual turnover in a small business varies between R3 million in the agricultural sector and R13 million in the manufacturing and catering, accommodation and other trade sectors, with a maximum of R32 million in the wholesale trade sector. The upper limits for employment and turnover of small businesses in the various sectors are shown in Table 1.1.

TABLE 1.1: Definition of a small business according to industrial sector, employment and turnover

SECTOR OR SUBSECTOR IN ACCORDANCE WITH THE STANDARD INDUSTRIAL CLASSIFICATION	THE TOTAL FULL-TIME EQUIVALENT OF PAID EMPLOYEES	TOTAL TURNOVER
Agriculture	50	R3m
Mining and Quarrying	50	R10m
Manufacturing	50	R13m
Electricity, Gas and Water	50	R13m
Construction	50	R6m
Retail and Motor Trade, and Repair Services	50	R19m
Wholesale Trade, Commercial Agents and Allied Services	50	R32m
Catering, Accommodation and other trade	50	R6m
Transport, Storage and Communications	50	R13m
Finance and Business Services	50	R13m
Community, Social and Personal Services	50	R6m

1.3.2 The formal medium business

Small businesses sometimes grow to become medium businesses when it is a truly entrepreneurial business. Medium businesses employ between 50 and 200 employees, with turnover from the upper limit of small businesses as indicated in Table 1.1. Medium businesses are highly formalised and require special professional expertise, management and of course a dedicated entrepreneur or entrepreneurial team.

Successful entrepreneurs inspire and act as role models. There are many exceptional entrepreneurs such as the late Steve Jobs of Apple, Mark Zuckerberg of Facebook, now Meta, and Elon Musk (an ex-South African) of Tesla Motors and SpaceX. The list includes many South Africans such as Patrice Motsepe of African Rainbow Minerals (ARM); Richard Maponya of Maponya Mall; Raymond Ackerman of Pick n Pay; Herman Mashaba of

Black Like Me; and Jannie Mouton of PSG, a financial services group. But there are many lesser-known people with whom we can more easily identify. Examples of their businesses exist in all economic sectors, and vary from micro businesses in basic products and services to sophisticated IT companies and highly professional practices. Some examples in the small and medium (and growing) business category presented in Example 1.3.

EXAMPLE 1.3

1. Kimberley Taylor identified a problem in logistics companies. The sector seemed to be low tech and they managed their drivers in a very basic manner, using pegboards. She established her business Loop that is an integrated system that connects delivery companies with everyone, such as suppliers and customers, involved in their operations. The system consists of various apps that are customised to the needs of each of Loops's client businesses. Since the start-up of Loop in 2017 the company has grown to 12 people in 2022, soon to increase to 16 employees. Checkers, RTT, Nando's and Servest are only some of Loop's client companies. Loop has played a prominent role in the success of Checkers' Sixty60 delivery app (Shevel, 2022).

2. On his 40th birthday in 2011, Andy Reid decided to spoil himself and buy a Vespa scooter. When he could not find a new one anywhere in South Africa, he went to Italy – and returned with 600 Vespas. Today he is head of Vespa South Africa. According to Reid, the business started from a very low base and began to break even only after seven years.

   Vespa is an iconic, timeless brand. In addition to selling scooters and accessories, Vespa also provides customers with lessons in driving two-wheel vehicles, assists them in acquiring motor bike licences and provides delivery scooters to businesses. Currently, Vespa has branches in Johannesburg, Cape Town and Durban (Jonker, 2015:17).

3. Entrepreneurs do not always start a completely new business, but often explore and identify new markets and open businesses to service them. Big Blue, the clothing and lifestyle business of Philip Cronje and James Robertson, started off as a flea-market stall in 1986. The two needed a form of escape from their full-time corporate jobs and decided to go on their own. Fortunately, frequent travelling was part of their respective corporate jobs and exposed them to creative ideas and people.

   With limited access to interesting and different fabrics, they created and designed their own fabrics for their clothes that eventually became an iconic range of prints, crafts and designs. During 2003, they opened their first store in Centurion and are now the owners of an interesting, quirky and sustainable, proudly South African business with 21 stores selling clothes made from unique fabrics as well as collections of South African memorabilia.

   Their range of products includes ladies' and men's clothing, bags, homeware and interesting gifts. Some products are cheap copies and others recycled and produced by crafting groups such as a Hillcrest Aids project, Diepsloot crafters and anyone who produces products that catch their attention. Through Big Blue many entrepreneurs have market success. The jobs created and maintained by Big Blue include those of their suppliers and service providers (Viktor, 2015:12; Big Blue, 2018).

4. Peter Herrmann, a textile engineer, and his wife, Coba, started Hertex (Herrmann Textiles) in 1987 in a shed in an industrial area of Cape Town with their first fabric showroom. Although the initial product was fabric, they have expanded and their products, primarily for the décor market, now include fabrics for upholstery, curtaining and drapery; floor and wall coverings; throws and cushion inners. They expanded Hertex to include HAUS, a homeware collection consisting of occasional furniture and tableware. Currently, there are 14 Hertex showrooms and Hertex is the largest local company in the industry. In addition, Hertex operates internationally through agents and has a showroom in London.

The company houses a variety of brands serving different niche markets including Stonehaus, faBella, Couture, Padari and Studio H.

Hertex is a true entrepreneurial family business as their three daughters are also operational, sales and human resource directors of the business. The family also owns and successfully operates two farms, Edelweiss and Bella Montaña, in the Piketberg area, growing food and indigenous flowers for export to international markets (Van der Merwe, 2015:80; Hertex, 2022).

LO 4: Explain corporate entrepreneurship/intrapreneurship

1.4 Corporate entrepreneurship, or intrapreneurship

Corporate entrepreneurship, or intrapreneurship, is also a form of entrepreneurship. It occurs when the corporate entrepreneur identifies a specific business opportunity and establishes a new business within the structure of an existing one.

DEFINITION   Corporate entrepreneurship (also known as intrapreneurship) is the creation of a business or businesses within an existing large business, using new ideas and exploiting opportunities. The new and relatively small autonomous business unit produces a product or service using the resources of an existing business.

Corporate entrepreneurship makes it possible for large businesses to adapt to changes in the market entrepreneurially; experiment in the market; diversify from the core business; establish new distribution channels; and make profits from new businesses.

EXAMPLE 1.4

An example of corporate entrepreneurship is First National Bank (FNB), which used to be a conventional bank. FNB ventured into new businesses such as Outsurance and Discovery Health.

Outsurance is a short-term insurance company and represents diversification of FNB's core, traditional business. Outsurance itself was innovative in offering direct, short-term insurance to individuals without the traditional intermediary insurance brokers. Outsurance has grown from a small corporate entrepreneurial business to a large insurance business.

Discovery Health is another corporate entrepreneurship venture, established by a corporate entrepreneur, Adrian Gore, within FNB during the 1990s. It grew to become the largest and most innovative independent medical aid group in South Africa, and has expanded internationally.

Another development of a corporate venture is Discovery Bank out of Discovery. Discovery, now a leader in insurance in South Africa, entered retail banking with Discovery Bank in 2018. Discovery's success was built its on its medical insurance business, Discovery Health.

1.4.1 Franchisors and franchisees

DEFINITION   Franchising is an arrangement in which an individual or business (the franchisor) grants an independent party (the franchisee) the right to sell the products or services of the business according to guidelines set down by the franchisor.

The franchisor retains control over the conduct of the business and offers the franchisee a comprehensive business package. Examples of franchises are Nando's, Cash Converters, King Pie, Swarovski, Trellidor and Placecol Skin Care Clinics.

The franchisor is an entrepreneur, whereas the franchisee should rather be seen as a corporate entrepreneur (or intrapreneur) who innovates within the franchise system.

Franchisees do not have the latitude to experiment, operate and market their business according to their own vision of how things should be done, but must adhere to the plans of the franchisor. However, it has been proved that franchisees do show an entrepreneurial orientation in certain situations, such as multiple-outlet franchisees (Maritz, 2005). Franchisors in many sectors have recognised the benefit of multiple-unit franchisees (Johnson, 2004:3), and this is seen as an entrepreneurial extension of the franchise trend.

Franchisors usually fall into the medium- to large-business category, because the more successful franchisors manage a large number of franchises in addition to managing the franchising group. In South Africa alone there are 600 different franchise brands, up from only 156 in 1994. There are 31 000 franchise outlets operating in the country and 26% belong to previously disadvantaged groups. Franchises employ about 320 000 people. Approximately 25% of franchises in South Africa are fast-food restaurants and 13% are retail businesses responsible for 28% and 40% respectively of franchise business employment.

Franchisees can fall anywhere in the small to medium categories. Franchises represent a contribution of approximately 10% of GDP. Measured by sustainability, franchises are sound: 75% of franchises exist for more than six years and 44% remain in business for more than 12 (Brand-Jonker, 2015:2).

EXAMPLE 1.5

Nando's, the fast-food business serving food with a Mozambican/Portuguese theme, is a familiar South African name. This franchise was started by Robert Brozin and Fernando Duarte in Rosettenville, south of Johannesburg, in 1987 as a fast-food shop selling spicy, grilled chicken meals. By 2001, Nando's had 343 branches internationally and by 2017 this number had grown to more than 1 000 in 24 countries – a 190% increase – including Britain, Australia, the USA, Canada, Singapore, Malaysia, the Middle East and several African countries including Botswana, Namibia, Zambia, Zimbabwe and Mauritius. Many of the outlets are owned by Nando's itself (Nando's, 2017).

LO 5: Explain the key success factors of entrepreneurs

1.5　Key success factors of entrepreneurs

Entrepreneurs have distinctive characteristics. This does not mean that all entrepreneurs have the same characteristics or combinations of them. Some are successful because they are prepared to take chances, while others achieve their goals largely because of their innovative skills and flair for management. Each entrepreneur achieves success because of a unique combination of factors. In fact, research (Fillion, 1991; Timmons & Spinelli, 2009) has shown that there is no typical entrepreneur because few – if any – entrepreneurs possess all of the characteristics or skills discussed in this chapter.

Figure 1.1 summarises the key success factors that usually contribute to successful entrepreneurship.

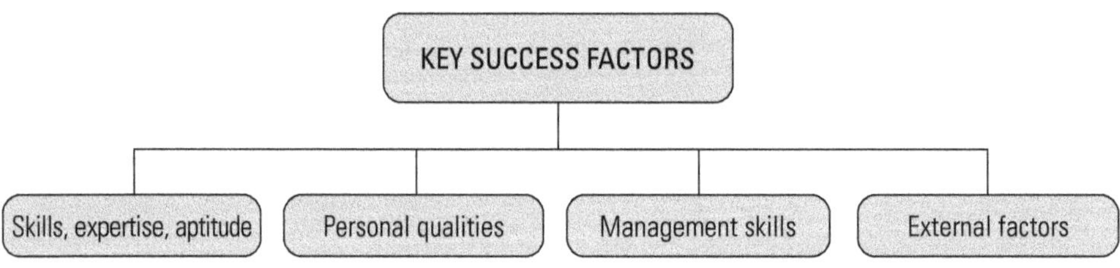

FIGURE 1.1: Key success factors

It is important for an entrepreneur to analyse their personal strengths and weaknesses. Their strengths can then be constructively applied and their weaknesses can be remedied by one or more of the following:

- personal development
- attending courses
- appointing staff and/or experts to compensate where needed.

1.5.1 The skills, expertise and aptitudes of an entrepreneur

Successful entrepreneurs have particular skills, expertise and aptitudes that can be applied profitably in any business. It is best to start or run a business with something you feel comfortable with and know a lot about (expertise) and/or in which you are skilled. The match between you, as the person starting the business, and the type of business is therefore most important.

DEFINITION Skills usually refer to manual work and can be learnt. You can learn to become, for example, an electrician, a hairdresser or a cabinet-maker.

Expertise is based on knowledge you acquire. Expertise and knowledge are obtained by studying and/or experience. There are experts in fields such as taxation, computer systems and study techniques.

Each person is also born with **aptitudes** and talents. Some are artistic, some have a talent for communicating, and others have a flair for figures.

EXAMPLE 1.6

The following are examples of ways in which an entrepreneur can use skills, expertise and aptitudes in specific businesses:

SKILLS, EXPERTISE AND APTITUDE REQUIRED BY BUSINESS TYPE	TYPE OF BUSINESS
Technical thinking (aptitude) + Knowledge of antiques (expertise) + Cabinet-maker (skill)	• Draws furniture designs • Restores antique furniture • Designs and installs kitchens and built-in cupboards
Artistic (aptitude) + Experience in jewellery design (expertise) + Apprentice in jewellery manufacture (skill)	• Produces and/or sells art • Designs jewellery • Manufactures jewellery
Analytical, practical thinking (aptitude) + Experience in stock control (expertise) + Knowledge of book retailing and of the need for reliable suppliers (skill)	• Develops computer programs • Develops methods of stock control for enterprises • Provides central distribution service for suppliers of books to retail shops

Usually, your skills, expertise and knowledge are a product of your natural aptitudes, talents and interests. Someone who has a strong verbal aptitude, for example, will learn languages easily and so develop a sound knowledge of languages with further study. People who are artistic can practise art as a career or a hobby. They could, for example, paint or be a graphic designer. Further study would enable them to qualify as an architect or jewellery designer.

The examples above illustrate how important it is for an entrepreneur to consider their skills, expertise and aptitudes when planning to start a business.

1.5.2 The important personal characteristics of entrepreneurs

Before discussing the personal characteristics of an entrepreneur, it is important to note that expertise, skills and aptitudes in isolation do not guarantee a successful business. To ensure success in your own business, business aptitude and management skills are indispensable. The following example highlights the range of skills necessary to manage an interior design business.

EXAMPLE 1.7

A successful interior decorator must have a thorough knowledge of materials, furniture styles and the use of space. Knowledge of various manufacturers and their products and services is also essential. Such a person must also be artistic and creative, with a feel for colour and dimensions to be able to furnish a room tastefully. These are the person's expertise and talents. The interior decorator must also maintain sound human relations, because they will deal with many different people (clients, employees, suppliers and the public) when the business is marketed.

By staying personally involved in the business, the entrepreneur will use their expertise and talents to offer clients the best possible service. This in turn ensures the success of the business.

The following personal characteristics are important to ensure the success of an entrepreneur.

Perseverance

Entrepreneurs have confidence in themselves and their businesses and carry on in spite of setbacks, difficult situations and problems. They are able to take immediate decisions, but can also exercise patience until a task has been completed and a goal reached. They do not lose heart when they make mistakes or fail.

Successful entrepreneurs have an intense determination and a need to overcome obstacles, solve problems and complete a task. They are not intimidated by difficult situations.

Commitment to the business

Entrepreneurs dedicate their skills, expertise and resources to establishing and building the business. They prove their commitment by:

- using their own money to establish the business
- taking a mortgage on a house
- working long hours in order to succeed
- accepting a lower standard of living and possibly earning little or no income from the business until it is successful.

Involvement in the business

Entrepreneurs are personally involved in their business and are aware of everything that is happening on all levels and in all sections of the business. They perform tasks themselves and communicate well with staff and others involved with the business, such as suppliers and clients. The example of the interior decorator reminds us of the importance of personal involvement.

Willingness to take risks

Entrepreneurs take calculated risks. This means that the risk related to a business opportunity must not be too great, for then the chance of success is not in the hands of the entrepreneur. They are not gamblers. The level of risk should not be too low either, for then exploiting the opportunity does not pose a challenge and is usually not as profitable. A risk factor that is too low implies limited profitability. A business opportunity with a low risk factor makes it easy to enter the market, but also increases the risks of competition. In the business world this consideration is called 'barriers to entry'.

Entrepreneurs usually try to reduce risk by finding investors to provide finance, making arrangements with suppliers to provide goods on consignment or persuading suppliers to accept special payment terms, and so forth. The successful entrepreneur will carefully plan and consider each business opportunity.

Sound human relations

Entrepreneurs work closely with other people: they realise they cannot be successful in isolation and therefore motivate their employees. They not only know how to build contacts and long-term relationships to benefit their business, but also how to stay on good terms with suppliers, clients and others involved in the business.

Successful entrepreneurs realise the importance of business relationships. They have good relations with clients, see human relations as an important resource of the enterprise and regard long-term goodwill as more important than short-term benefits. Sound human relations have been identified as one factor that differentiates the 'successful' entrepreneur from the 'average' in developing countries (McClelland, 1986).

Successful and average entrepreneurs maintain good personal relations by, for example, using strategies to develop business contacts and influential people to achieve their goals. They are able to persuade people to buy a product or service or to provide financing. They use their capabilities, reliability and other personal or business qualities (McClelland, 1986).

Creativity and innovative ability

In this context, 'creativity' refers to a person's imagination and ability to think creatively. Creativity involves generating new and useable ideas to solve any problem or exploit any opportunity. In the long term, an enterprise's success is determined by the degree to which good ideas are generated, developed and implemented. Creativity consists of people being open to new ideas and new approaches to the business, and focusing on what can be done differently to ensure success in the business. In other words, effective entrepreneurs take the initiative to solve problems in a unique manner. Innovative ability refers more to the use of creative abilities to create something concrete. So it is logical that creative thinking, but especially innovative ability, is fundamental to starting a new enterprise.

Creativity distinguishes an entrepreneur from their competitors. Often it does not represent a radically new method, but it may be a method that satisfies a client's need in a better way.

Positive attitude and approach

Entrepreneurs learn from their setbacks and failures. They are realistic and accept that disappointments are inevitable, and are not discouraged when these occur. They are able to identify opportunities even in adverse and difficult situations.

All this indicates that entrepreneurs remain positive despite setbacks, failure and disappointment. This does not mean they do not sometimes feel dispirited when events are not favourable, but on the whole they manage situations well. We often read of entrepreneurs who, having lost everything, sometimes more than once, start afresh. Success is achieved by using negative experiences positively and learning from past mistakes.

EXAMPLE 1.8

Henry Ford, father of the motor car assembly line and the first mass-produced motor car (the Model T Ford), twice started enterprises (both times building racing cars) that proved unsuccessful, before achieving success.

1.5.3 The important functional management skills of entrepreneurs

The management skills of an entrepreneur are an indication of how well the entrepreneur can perform important tasks or activities. Related activities are grouped, and are known as the eight functions of a business (see Figure 1.2).

The functions are described in more detail in Chapter 2 and Chapter 6, where they are applied as part of setting up a business.

In this section, which is about you, the entrepreneur, your ability to perform specific activities in the enterprise is discussed. Every entrepreneur must be aware of their strengths and weaknesses when it comes to management skills in the various business functions, so that they can apply or supplement them to build a successful enterprise.

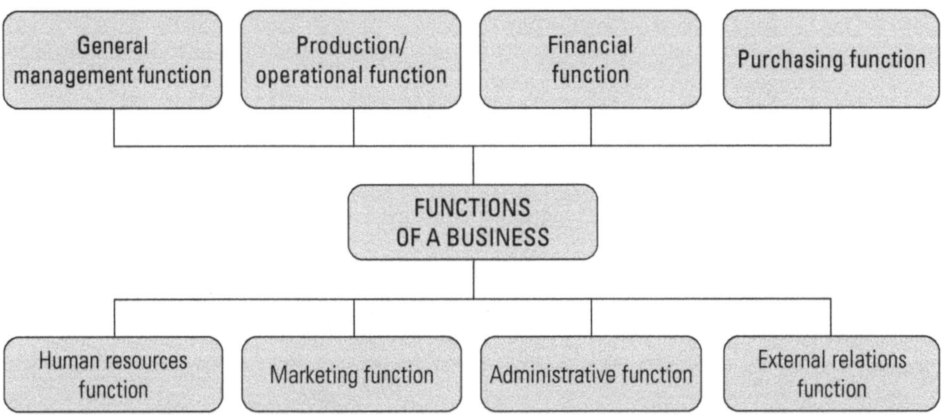

FIGURE 1.2: The eight functions of a business

If you think back to the example of the interior decorator, it is evident that the success of a business demands specific management skills.

EXAMPLE 1.9

The interior decorator must be market oriented. She must know which target market is to be served, for example:

- the higher-income group or corporate clients
- people with modern, traditional or alternative tastes.

According to management consultants, marketing expertise and management expertise are essential for the successful operation of SMMEs. Thus, the entrepreneur should have a minimum or particular combination of these management skills.

The decorator must also be familiar with marketing methods and know how to reach the target market. Managing the income and applying funds are equally essential for the survival and profitability of the business. If the interior decorator cannot manage her finances, she will have to get expert assistance.

IMPORTANT INFORMATION

The following important aspects of management skills will be discussed below:

- planning a business before it is established
- general management skills and the use of advisers
- customer service
- knowledge of competitors
- market orientation
- the importance of quality products or services
- accounting for your own purposes
- insight into expenditure, income, profit and loss
- the ability to use income wisely.

Planning a business before it is established

This activity is part of the general management function and involves drawing up the business plan. A well-considered business plan ensures that the business is launched with confidence; a plan shows that the necessary research and planning have been done.

Entrepreneurs often do the planning very informally because there is no time to draw up a formal business plan, or simply because they do not know how to do it. Despite their informal planning, these entrepreneurs can be successful.

IMPORTANT INFORMATION

Formal planning and drawing up a business plan are desirable activities because they enable the entrepreneur to:

- identify problems early on so that they can make wise decisions and fewer mistakes
- consider all the important factors of the intended business and, in so doing, become free of purely instinctive or crisis decisions, thus avoiding stress
- take decisions for the future
- use this planning stage as an ideal opportunity for testing ideas.

The guidelines for developing a business plan are provided in Chapter 5.

General management skills and the use of advisers

Entrepreneurs must know what is needed for success in a specific business and must be intent on developing their skills in these critical areas of performance. If marketing the business's products is the critical area of performance, and a significant determinant of the success of the enterprise, the entrepreneur must know how to carry out this function. If they do not have the necessary expertise, trained staff should be appointed. The entrepreneur should also understand the environment in which they are competing and be well organised. Know-how is often more important than creativity.

As an entrepreneur, it is logical that you will start a business in which you can use the strengths of expertise and skill. You will also usually be aware of (or soon discover) your weaknesses. Then you can strengthen or supplement your weak areas by:

- using other people, such as employees, consultants, contractors or professional experts
- working on your self-development and consciously remedying deficiencies by learning from others, attending courses, reading or studying.

EXAMPLE 1.10

The interior decorator knows that she is a creative, artistic and stylish person. She realises that her financial knowledge is insufficient for her to do her own accounting, and therefore outsources this to an accountant. As a good businesswoman she accepts that she must be able to understand financial statements, and therefore takes a course to learn the basic financial terms and principles to inform her proper business decisions. She has identified her weaknesses, and is taking steps to avoid having her enterprise harmed by them.

Customer service

This activity is included in the marketing and administrative functions. Entrepreneurs who maintain good human relations are aware of clients' needs, and so provide very good customer service. Examples are after-sales service; attention to detail, such as serving refreshments when a client visits; personal presentability and attractive premises; user-friendliness; and having a neatly ordered shop and clear instructions for using products. Clients remember, support and recommend a business that meets their needs and gives them something extra without making them feel they are paying for it. Little gestures mean a lot: a balloon or sticker for the child; a cup of tea or glass of champagne in the jewellery store; changing an order on short notice; or just friendly, helpful service.

Administrative and technical factors are also crucial to sound customer service. Keep accurate records and an up-to-date filing system for reference and stock control. Use a diary so that you can plan your time and keep appointments, and document client information for easy reference. These are a few examples of methods to ensure effective customer service.

Knowledge of competitors

This activity is also part of the marketing function. Successful entrepreneurs know:

- who their competitors are
- how many competitors they have
- the size of their competitors' operations
- which segment of the market their competitors control
- the quality of their competitors' products or services
- how to distinguish themselves from their competitors and so ensure and increase their visibility and thus their share of the market
- how to establish their competitors' strengths and weaknesses, thus converting a competitor's weakness into an opportunity for their own business.

EXAMPLE 1.11

An entrepreneur sells various artists' work: he knows his competitors and distinguishes his business by going out to visit clients at their homes or places of work with a truck full of art work, rather than expecting them to come to his art gallery. He takes along a variety of suitable works of art to make the client's choice easier. His professional knowledge of art, its quality and his taste and flair for colour and style (talent) are presented to the client in a unique fashion. Clients are able to view the art work where they plan to display it. He is successful because his competitors sell their products from art galleries, shops or at auctions, with no apparent interest in the client's home or place of work.

Market orientation

Market orientation also forms part of the marketing function. Successful entrepreneurs are market-oriented. They know who or what their target market is; its demands and needs; and how to meet these needs profitably. (The example of the interior decorator illustrates this functional skill.) A market-conscious entrepreneur has developed products and services to satisfy the client's requirements.

A market-conscious entrepreneur is positioned realistically in relation to competitors. This means that the entrepreneur's products and/or services are distinguished (by look, feel, design, packaging, price, delivery mechanism and online presence) from competitors' to ensure profitability and a competitive edge. The customer is the focus of the business, and products and/or services are developed and adapted to meet the client's desires as well as needs.

Product-oriented entrepreneurs often have problems because they are more concerned with the product than the client, and consequently do not know how to market their products/services successfully.

The following should serve as a warning:

> **IMPORTANT INFORMATION**
>
> Many aspiring entrepreneurs are so in love with their product-service idea that they ignore the market; they assume their product or service will sell. The market road is strewn with product-service ideas that were heavily, and many times cleverly, advertised and went bust (Burch, 1986:79).

The importance of quality products or services

This activity is part of both the marketing and purchasing functions. Quality products are not necessarily expensive products. However, the client expects the quality of the product to be consistent with the price charged. Value for money is important. A successful entrepreneur aims to offer clients a quality product while still remaining profitable. Costs must be kept in check without affecting the quality of goods. Quality products and services contribute to marketing, as they generate new clients through personal recommendations by existing, satisfied clients.

Accounting for your own purposes

This activity is part of the administrative and financial function. Successful entrepreneurs realise that they must be able to understand their own accounting systems. Simplicity and usefulness are the most important features of these systems.

A simple system that suits the business is essential. The entrepreneur must understand what has to be done and why, so that the information provided can be properly used. If the size and complexity of an enterprise are such that the accounting cannot be done internally, a qualified person must be appointed for this function or it can be outsourced to another person or company. The usefulness of the information provided by the accounting system is of cardinal importance because it allows the entrepreneur to make decisions on how to improve the management of the enterprise.

Insight into expenditure, income, profit and loss

This activity is part of the financial function. Successful entrepreneurs distinguish between income and profit. They realise that income must first be used to buy new stock, to pay creditors, wages, salaries and tax, and for current expenses. Only once this has been done can the entrepreneur determine what portion of the remaining income or profit can be ploughed back into the business and how much can be used for personal remuneration. The entrepreneur knows how to calculate profit and what it means to show a loss. They must know which costs are essential and understand the implication of increased expenses. This management skill is closely related to the next skill, namely the ability to use income wisely.

The ability to use income wisely

This activity is also part of the financial function. We discussed this management skill in the example of the interior decorator.

The successful entrepreneur exercises financial discipline and understands what to spend on to ensure success. An expensive car conveys an image of success, or it may be a source of resentment or suspicion to the customer. If this will serve the business, the entrepreneur may take the risk of buying the car. On the other hand, a successful entrepreneur will not waste money on unnecessary personal luxuries and status symbols.

Entrepreneurs must constantly take decisions on expenses. They must develop the ability to make the right decisions to ensure growth.

IMPORTANT INFORMATION

Examples of good decisions are:

- collecting outstanding payments of clients as soon as possible
- postponing the payment of a debt/creditor for as long as possible to keep cash available for a special offer on necessary stocks, which will enhance profitability
- applying profits to the business instead of spending them on holidays, luxuries or a more expensive house or car
- using money wisely in departments or on products that will result in the greatest profitability for the enterprise.

Remember that although all management skills are important, few – if any – entrepreneurs have all the management skills necessary to run a successful business.

LO 6: Explain how entrepreneurs should deal with external factors that affect their business

1.6   Dealing with external factors that affect the business

External factors and circumstances also influence the way an entrepreneur may be able to exploit their potential, and the potential of the business. How you accommodate, deal with and even exploit external factors to your personal advantage is a measure of your entrepreneurship.

IMPORTANT INFORMATION

As an entrepreneur you must be aware of the following external factors:

- **Economic conditions**
  The entrepreneur must know how to adapt to fluctuating interest rates or declining levels of customer spending power.

- **Technological changes**
  The entrepreneur must keep up with technological developments and know how to exploit them to the benefit of their business. For example, digitalise some of the business functions, create an online presence and/or expand into e-commerce.

- **Social and cultural forces**
  The entrepreneur must be able to identify opportunities for growth in market share, given the fact that large sectors of the population are now better educated.

- **Political and legislative variables**
  The entrepreneur must realise the opportunities that arise after political adjustments and events.

- **Physical variables**
  The entrepreneur must keep abreast of the availability and price of resources, such as considering the use of alternative raw materials if prices rise.

- **International forces**
  The entrepreneur who uses technologically advanced communication channels can, for example, expand to and even establish a business in another country.

These external factors are discussed fully in Chapter 2.

1.7 Summary

Competencies, expertise, aptitude, personal characteristics and management skills determine how a person will handle external factors. The relationship between a person's inherent attributes and external factors is crucial to successful entrepreneurship.

The importance of entrepreneurial business at all levels is essential to a country's economic development, wealth and employment creation. Entrepreneurship was identified as a specialised discipline that can be taught and learnt. Entrepreneurial development is the origin of successful entrepreneurial activity, and although some are born entrepreneurs, it is possible to develop individuals to become entrepreneurs. This is where entrepreneurial education and training play an important role.

The entrepreneur who applies certain talents, skills and expertise in the start-up, development and growth of a business was introduced as a person who continuously creates and innovates to build and develop a business of recognisable value.

Many entrepreneurs start small businesses, but then prefer to remain small due to lifestyle preferences. Small businesses are usually owner-managed with limited employees, but, although not entrepreneurial, are also very valuable contributors to the economy of a country.

Entrepreneurs are found in a variety of types of businesses, including formal small, micro and medium businesses, as franchisors or franchisees, or within other businesses as corporate entrepreneurs.

All the success factors including the competencies, expertise, aptitude, personal qualities, management skills and external factors that have been discussed must be analysed in personal terms. This may discourage some potential entrepreneurs, but it is vital that the aspiring businessperson be aware of all the important aspects. Remember that a successful entrepreneur is self-critical, but optimistic about solving problems. The entrepreneur will, therefore, see which adjustments must be made or what can be done to start an enterprise that has been a dream. Thus, the entrepreneur has a vision. They realise that it is essential to evaluate realistically personal strengths and weaknesses in order to achieve goals.

Finally, the entrepreneur should be aware of the external factors such as economic conditions, technological changes, social and cultural forces, political and legislative variables, physical variables and international forces that influence a business.

SELF-EVALUATION QUESTIONS

1. Identify an entrepreneur and a small business owner in your community or reported on in the media. Describe both and indicate how the entrepreneur differs from the small business owner.

2. Can entrepreneurship be taught? Justify your answer.

3. Describe how entrepreneurs contribute to the national economy.

4. Using the example of the entrepreneur identified in Question 1 (or identifying another) describe what their business entails, and why you regard the person as an entrepreneur. Also indicate whether you regard the business as a micro, small or medium enterprise. Justify your classification.

5. Determine how a medium business differs from a small business.

6. Discuss the importance of the skills, expertise and aptitudes of an entrepreneur and determine your own skills, expertise and aptitudes.

7. List the seven personal characteristics that may contribute to successful entrepreneurship.

8. List and briefly describe the eight functional management skills of successful entrepreneurs.

REFERENCES AND FURTHER READING

Big Blue. 2018. About Big Blue. https://www.bigblue.co.za. (Accessed 31 May 2022).

Bird, BJ. 1989. *Entrepreneurial Behavior*. Glenview, IL: Scott, Foresman and Company.

Brand-Jonker, N. 2015. Franchises in Suid-Afrika. *Rapport*, 8 February 2015:2.

Burch, JG. 1986. *Entrepreneurship*. New York: John Wiley and Sons.

FASA. Franchise Association South Africa. 2015.

Fillion, LJ. 1991. From entrepreneurship to entreprenology: The emergence of a new discipline. *Journal of Enterprising Culture,* 6(1):1–24.

Gasparro, A. 2015. For Greek yogurt king, path isn't always smooth. *The Wall Street Journal*, 19 May 2015:10–11.

Global Entrepreneurship Monitor (GEM). 2021. Women's Entrepreneurship 2020/2021 Global Report. https://gemconsortium.org/report/gem-202021-womens-entrepreneurship-report-thriving-through-crisis. (Accessed 31 May 2022).

Hattingh, T. 2015. Onderneming pas en draai suksesvol. *SakeNuus*, 4 Mei 2015:12.

Hertex. 2022. http://www.hertex.co.za (Accessed 31 May 2022).

Johnson, DM. 2004. In the mainstream, multi-unit and multi-concept franchising, *Franchising World*, 36(3):3.

Jonker, S. 2015. Ikoniese bromponie stewig in die SA saal. *SakeNuus*, 15 April 2015.

Katz, J & Green, R. 2014. *Entrepreneurial Small Business*. New York: McGraw-Hill Irwin.

Kelly, JD. 2010. Seeing Red: Mao fetishism, Pax Americana, and the moral economy of war. In Kelly, JD, with Jaureguim B, Mitchell, ST, Walton, J. (eds). *Anthropology and Global Counterinsurgency*. Chicago: University of Chicago Press, 67–83.

Kerstiens, T. 1999. Pick a Color: Children of mixed race struggle to find identity. *Bellingham Herald*, 10 January:sc. C1.

Kongolo, M. 2010. Job creation versus job shedding and the role of small and medium enterprises in economic development. *African Journal of Business Management*, 4(11):2288–2295.

Kuratko, DF. 2014. *Entrepreneurship: Theory, Process, Practice*, 9th edition. Mason, Ohio: South-Western Cengage Learning.

Maritz, PA. 2005. Entrepreneurial service vision in a franchised home entertainment system. DCom thesis, University of Pretoria.

McClelland, DC. 1986. Characteristics of successful entrepreneurs. *Journal of Creative Behavior*, 21(3):219–233.

McClelland, DC. 1961. *The Achieving Society*. Princeton, NJ: Van Nostrand.

Nando's. 2017. Explore the Nando's world. https://www.nandos.com/worldwide/ (Accessed 31 May 2022).

Nieuwenhuizen, C & Kroon, J. 2002. Creating wealth by financing small and medium enterprises of owners who possess entrepreneurial skills. *Management Dynamics: Contemporary Research*, 11(1).

Schumpeter, JA. 1934. *The Theory of Economic Development*. Translated by R Opic. Cambridge, MA: Harvard University Press.

Shevel, A. 2015. Seat at top table for Steinhoff after years out in the cold. *Sunday Times Business*, 24 May: 3.

Shevel, A. 2022. In the Loop. *Financial Mail*. 17–23 February.

Timmons, JA & Spinelli, S. 2009. *New Venture Creation and Entrepreneurship*. 9th edition. Burr Ridge: Irwin.

Van der Merwe, L. 2015. Als in die familie. *Sarie*, April.

Viktor, A. 2015. Koel kurators en die konings van rondsnuffel. *Beeld*, 6 March.

Weinstein, JI. 2009. The Market in Plato's Republic. *Classical Philology*, 104:439–458.

Legislation

National Small Enterprise Act 102 of 1996 as amended by the National Small Business Amendment Act 26 of 2003.

National Small Enterprise Amendment Bill, 2020. *Government Gazette* 43981, 11 December.

BASIC BUSINESS CONCEPTS AND THE BUSINESS ENVIRONMENT

ANDREAS DE BEER

LEARNING OUTCOMES

After you have studied this chapter, you should be able to:

- LO 1: Explain the relationship between a business and an establishment
- LO 2: Discuss the classification of a business and its establishment in the economy
- LO 3: Explain the business environment

Introduction

In this chapter we are going to look at two important concepts: basic business concepts and principles, and the reason why the business environment is so important in the business world.

The first part of this chapter will look at the business as a need-satisfying organisation in the free-market system, and show the relationship between the business and the establishment. Second, the chapter will clarify how businesses are categorised into branches of industry and production. After the categorisation, we will explain the different sectors of the economy in which these entities operate and describe how raw materials and products move through these sectors to reach the consumer. (These are all basic business concepts.)

Lastly, we will show how enterprises survive by transforming ideas and opportunities from their business environment into goods and services that customers need and want to buy.

Consider whether it is possible for a business to exist in total isolation. Ask yourself if it is possible for a business to grow and exist if factors such as customers and their needs, competitor activity and prevailing economic and political conditions are not taken into consideration. The answer to these questions should be 'no': of course it is impossible for any business, large or small, to function in isolation. To be successful, a business must stay in constant contact with the environment so that it remains up to date with changing customer needs, changing technologies and competitor activities. If not, profitability may decline, putting the future of the business at risk.

EXAMPLE 2.1

In the music industry in 2001, CD album sales peaked in line with the dot-com bubble bursting. However, compact discs made vinyl almost obsolete, and are now rapidly being replaced by many different ways to transport and listen to music. Today, there are virtually hundreds of apps, websites and systems offering music streaming devices. For example, YouTube is famous for music videos – you can search for any song you like and most probably there will be some kind of video accompanying it. Spotify is an example of one of the most popular music streaming devices currently. You can listen to any song you want and you do not have to pay for it. The way they get around this is by making you listen to advertisements every couple of songs. A last example is Amazon's robot called Alexa – the one that can answer questions about the weather and whatnot. One of the most useful things that Alexa can do is to play music and podcasts. New technological developments or improvements such as these examples create definite opportunities for the business, but they may also constitute threats. The development of compact discs in the 1980s meant that long-playing records were no longer manufactured. Factories that used to manufacture tthem have been forced to change their strategies because of developments on the technological front. Currently compact disc producers are faced with new opportunities and threats of selling music through various digital channels. In addition, think of the continual changes in computer technology and the influence this has on banking, for example. New technologically improved products are constantly being introduced into the market.

EXAMPLE 2.2

Today's businesses function in an 'economy of ideas'. Never before in the history of business has so much change been introduced so quickly. Many of these changes are due to the changing business environment, in particular the rise of new communication technologies, multinational businesses and globalisation. The nature of the global economy has changed and just increasing production will not ensure growth. Technological change, coupled with the arrival of China in the international marketplace, created a situation in which the ability to manufacture at ever higher volume and lower cost is limited only by the market for the products themselves. Competition is reduced by the speed and power with which ideas spread online. The term 'millennials' refers to people who were born between 1982 and 1999. At present, this group constitutes the largest age group in the workforce. They generate new ideas, new ways of looking at issues, new behaviours and new viewpoints like concerns for social values. Therefore, the external and internal environment of every business is changing continuously and will affect every business.

Every business function exists within an environment (the business environment) where events and variables influence its activities. These events may pose opportunities or threats. Technological development is a good illustration (think about Example 2.1) of an opportunity or a threat. On the one hand, technology creates new opportunities because new products and services emerge. Technology will affect the way businesses communicate and how entrepreneurs learn and think. Entrepreneurs will be able to do and experience things that past generations could only dream of, but also force entrepreneurs to leave behind valued skills, practices and beliefs. Covid-19 has also influenced entrepreneurs to think differently and many people work remotely. Technology has been designed to help entrepreneurs and businesses to discover and expand markets for their services.

On the other hand, it can constitute a threat because it may result in products or services becoming obsolete.

IMPORTANT INFORMATION

As an entrepreneur, you must be aware of environmental variables and changes. With this knowledge, you can develop a plan of action to deal with potential opportunities or threats. Without this knowledge, your business will not grow or may cease to exist.

It is also important that you understand some basic business concepts, such as the role your business (or proposed business) plays in a free-market system; how different entities are categorised into branches of industry and production; the different sectors of the economy; and how raw materials and products move through these sectors to reach the customer.

LO 1: Explain the relationship between a business and an establishment

2.1 The relationship between a business and an establishment

DEFINITION A business or enterprise can be described as an independent institution established by an entrepreneur to make a profit by producing goods or providing services that satisfy customers' needs. Therefore, the entrepreneur identifies a customer need and creates a business to produce goods and/or provide services to satisfy that need. The motive for the entrepreneur's action is to make a profit. Both parties, the entrepreneur and the customer, benefit from the creation of the business: the customer's needs are satisfied, while the entrepreneur makes a profit.

DEFINITION The establishment can be described as the place where inputs such as raw materials and other components are processed to produce a product or provide a service. Production activities take place in the establishment.

The best way of explaining the relationship between the business and the establishment is to look at Figure 2.1. This figure illustrates the shoe manufacturing business started by Tumi Lekoto (an entrepreneur).

Tumi combines the production factors of natural resources, capital, labour and entrepreneurship in his business. Tumi (the entrepreneur) will employ people to work for him (labour). He will also use capital to buy the raw materials (natural resources) he needs to manufacture the shoes.

Once the production process is complete, the end product (shoes) can be sold using marketing activities to generate income for Tumi's business. He will also use the external relations activities to improve the image of his business. The general management and administrative functions will oversee all the activities.

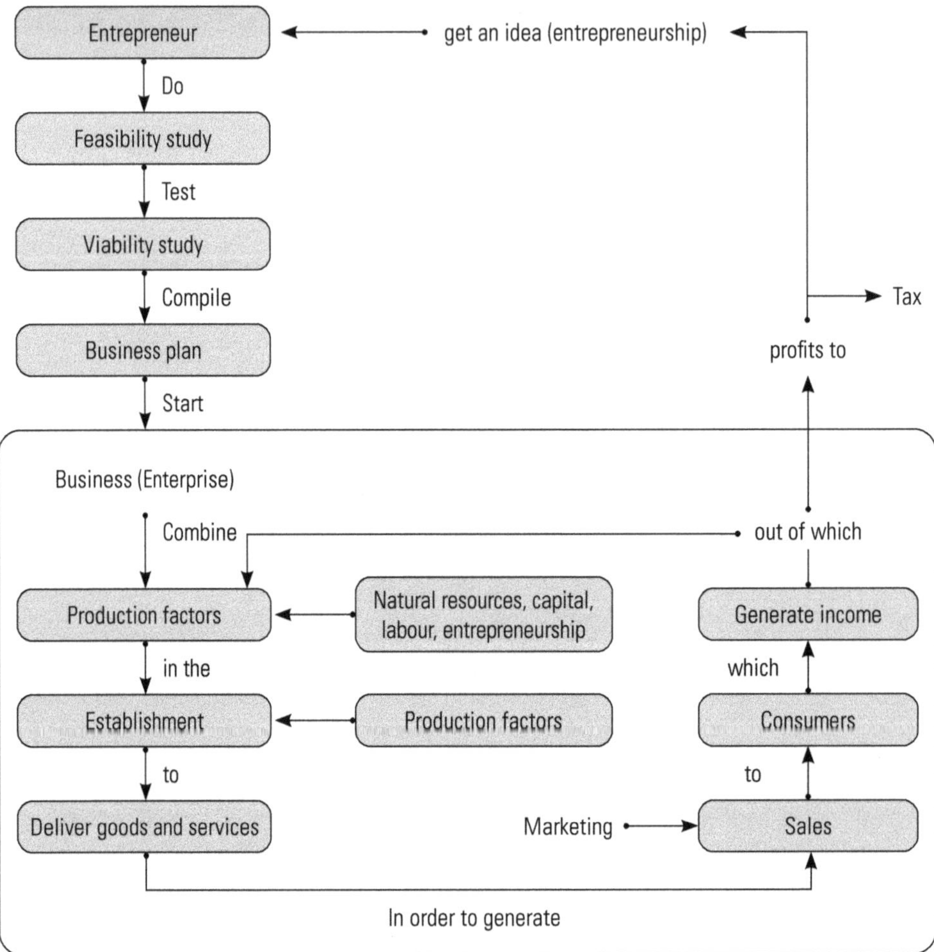

FIGURE 2.1: Relationship between the enterprise and its establishment

IMPORTANT INFORMATION

The establishment is a part of the business. The 'business' or 'enterprise' is the place where all the business functions take place (for example, marketing, management, administration), but the establishment refers only to the place where the product is made or the service provided.

LO 2: Discuss the classification of a business and its establishment in the economy

2.2 Classification of a business and its establishment in the economy

2.2.1 The branch of industry and the production branch

The difference between a branch of industry and the production branch is illustrated in Table 2.1.

TABLE 2.1: Branch of industry versus production branch

BRANCH OF INDUSTRY	PRODUCTION BRANCH
A branch of industry refers to all the businesses that produce more or less the same product or provide the same service. For example: Gold mines produce the same product, namely gold.	The production branch refers to all the businesses that use more or less the same production processes. For example: All mines – gold, diamond and coal mines – form part of the mining production branch, because they all use the same production process, namely extracting natural resources through mining.

2.2.2 The different sectors in which a business can operate

The activities occurring in the establishment determine the operating sector. There are five sectors in which a business can operate, namely the primary, secondary, tertiary, quarternity and quinary sectors:

1. **Primary sector:** This is responsible for the exploitation of natural resources in their raw, unprocessed form. Activities associated with primary economic activity include agriculture, mining, forestry, hunting and gathering, fishing and quarrying.

2. **Secondary sector:** In the secondary sector, the exploited natural resources are processed and transformed into products demanded by customers. Activities associated with the secondary sector include metalworking and smelting, automobile production, textile production, the chemical and engineering industries, aerospace manufacturing, energy utilities, breweries and bottlers, construction and shipbuilding.

3. **Tertiary sector:** This sector is responsible for distributing the final products from the manufacturer to the customer. Activities associated with this sector include retail and wholesale sales, transportation and distribution, restaurants, clerical services, media, tourism, insurance, banking, health care and law.

4. **Quaternary sector:** The fourth sector of the economy, the quaternary sector, comprises intellectual activities often associated with technological innovation. It is sometimes called the knowledge economy. Activities associated with this sector include government, culture, libraries, scientific research, education and information technology. These intellectual services and activities are what drive technological advancement, which can have a huge impact on short- and long-term economic growth.

5. **Quinary sector:** This sector comprises the highest levels of decision-making in a society or economy. This sector includes top executives or officials in such fields as government, science, universities, nonprofits, health care, culture and the media. It may also include police and fire departments, which are public services as opposed to for-profit enterprises. Economists sometimes also include domestic activities (duties performed in the home by a family member or dependant) in the quinary sector. These activities, such as childcare or housekeeping, are typically not measured by monetary amounts but contribute to the economy by providing services for free that would otherwise be paid for.

2.2.3 The industrial column

DEFINITION	The industrial column is the course that a product takes from its unprocessed, natural resource state to the final form in which it is supplied to the customer. This includes all the processes and transactions that occur from the primary sector, through the secondary sector and along to the tertiary sector, where the product is passed on to the customer.

Figure 2.2 illustrates the industrial column, using the manufacturing and distribution of paper as an example.

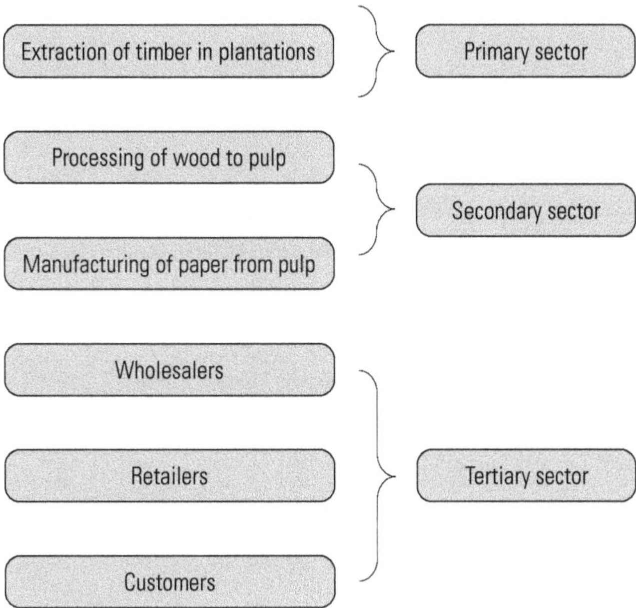

FIGURE 2.2: The industrial column

LO 3: Explain the business environment

2.3 The business environment

> **DEFINITION** The business environment is the sum of all the factors and variables that influence the creation, growth and continued existence of the business either positively or negatively, thereby promoting or hindering the achievement of its objectives.

The effect of the business environment on a business will be determined by the place and role of the business in the total economy of a country. The business environment has several characteristics:

- **Interrelatedness of environmental factors or variables:** A change in one external factor may cause a change in the micro environment and, similarly, a change in one external factor may influence other external environmental variables. A practical example is the instability and fluctuation of the value of the rand against the dollar, pound and other currencies. A drastic fall in the value of the rand means that imported goods such as cars and fuel become more expensive. This initially results in inflationary pressures, which are followed by high interest rates to contain the inflation. This in turn means that consumer spending declines and that certain industries suffer.

- **Increasing instability:** The interdependence between environmental factors results in increasing instability and change in the environment. Even if there is a general increase in the rate of change in the environment, environmental fluctuations are greater for some businesses than for others.
- **Environmental uncertainty:** This is a function of the amount of information available on environmental variables. There are both opportunities and threats in the business environment. Opportunities and threats arise as a result of certain occurrences in the environment and they influence the functioning of the business. An opportunity is a favourable situation for the business. The business must decide how to react to these opportunities and threats.
- **Complexity of the environment:** This characteristic indicates the number of external variables to which the business must react, as well as fluctuations in the variables themselves. The business management environment changes constantly. Factors that influence the business today will not necessarily have the same influence tomorrow. A good example is the rapid change in technology over the last few years.
- **Unpredictability of the environment:** The current business environment is revolutionary, which is unpredictable and is characterised by discontinuous change. The business must be in step with the changing environment. During the past few years, environmental emphasis has increasingly been placed on the protection of the ozone layer and this has resulted in businesses having to adapt their products accordingly.

The business environment is usually divided into three components, namely the micro environment (the internal environment), the market environment and the macro environment (both part of the external environment). Each component has various variables (see Table 2.2) that can either benefit or harm the business. (These are discussed in the sections that follow.) Figure 2.3 gives an overall picture of the business environment. The business is identified as the central point in this figure.

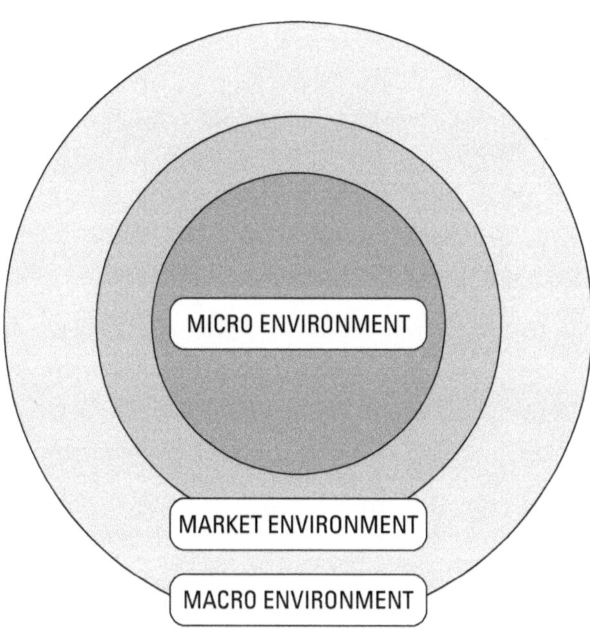

FIGURE 2.3:The internal and external business environment

TABLE 2.2: The components and variables of the business environment

THE MICRO ENVIRONMENT

This is the business itself. We can distinguish between the following variables:

- the mission statement and objectives of the business
- the functions of the business
- the production factors of the business.

THE MARKET ENVIRONMENT

This surrounds the business and is part of the external environment. The main variables include:

- the market
- the competition
- the suppliers of resources and services (without which the business would not be able to manufacture and market its products and/or provide services).

2.3.1 The micro environment

The micro environment is the heart of the business. It indicates to what extent the business is able to utilise opportunities or oppose threats in the external environment.

DEFINITION The micro environment is the sum of factors and variables which occur internally in the business, and are influenced directly or indirectly by management decisions. These factors and variables have a fundamental influence on the establishment, growth and continued existence of the business.

The micro environment consists of the following variables:

The mission statement and objectives of the business

This is what the business hopes to achieve and how it intends to do so. The mission statement and objectives must correspond with the demands of the external environment.

The functions of the business

The functions of the business include the following management divisions:

- general management
- human resource management
- operations
- logistics
- purchasing
- marketing
- public relations
- information management
- finance.

IMPORTANT INFORMATION

General management: General management differs from the other functions in that it does not occur in a separate department. General management deals with all the activities that are necessary to the task of management on all levels and throughout the entire organisation.

Human resource management: Human resource management includes all activities concerned with the procurement, development, compensation, integration and maintenance of the personnel of the organisation.

Operations management: Operations management refers to the management process used in both manufacturing and service enterprises. It can be described as those management activities that take place to ensure that products and services can be provided to satisfy the needs of the consumer.

Logistics management: Logistics management is responsible for planning, implementing and controlling the efficient flow and storage of goods, services and related information in order to meet customers' requirements.

Purchasing management: The purchasing management function deals with procuring the resources an organisation needs to meet its objectives. This includes determining purchasing needs, establishing alternative suppliers who can satisfy these needs and negotiating agreements with suppliers to the long-term advantage of the organisation.

Marketing management: Marketing is the process of transferring goods and services to meet and satisfy customer needs, and those activities that make this transfer possible. Marketing management, therefore, entails more than just advertising products and services: it includes a variety of activities that cut across all functions of the enterprise.

Public relations management: Public relations is the management function that researches, defines and evaluates public attitudes and seeks to align the business to them. It identifies the policies and procedures of an individual or organisation with a public interest, and plans and executes a programme of action to earn public acceptance and understanding.

Information management: This function can be defined as being concerned with the service of obtaining, recording and analysing information, and communicating the results to management, who then can safeguard the assets, promote the activities and achieve the organisation's objectives.

Financial management: Financial management refers to the management of the business's financial activities. The financial functions therefore include all the activities involved in obtaining capital and using it efficiently. The financial manager is responsible for planning, organising and controlling the financial activities in the organisation.

The production factors of the business

The production factors of the business include the resources available to a business, such as labour, raw materials (eg minerals, timber and water), capital and entrepreneurship. With these resources the business must use opportunities to ward off threats in the external environment. For example, if a business has sufficient capital available, new markets and new products can be explored. On the other hand, a lack of capital may constitute a threat to the business if its market position is weaker than that of its competitors.

The influence of management on the micro environment

As the manager of your own business, you will exert a direct influence on the mission statement and objectives of the business. You will decide where the business is going and what it will do to get there, and establish guidelines for its day-to-day operation.

The micro environment is the heart of a business. It also indicates to what extent a business is able to utilise opportunities or withstand threats in the external environment. Although the business can influence the internal environment by means of decision-making, it does not possess all the internal resources needed to handle opportunities and threats from the external environment. This confirms our point of departure that a business cannot function, grow or survive in a vacuum.

2.3.2   The market environment

The market can be defined as the link between the business and the environment in which it functions, and which surrounds the micro environment.

DEFINITION	The market environment is the sum of all the external factors and/or variables that may not be subject to control, but can sometimes be influenced to benefit the business.

The market environment is surrounded by the macro environment (see Figure 2.3 earlier in this chapter). The market environment, therefore, does not exist in isolation but is in fact influenced by both the micro and macro environments, as explained in Example 2.3.

EXAMPLE 2.3

- A new shampoo is introduced to the market. Customers prefer this new shampoo to the existing products made by competitors.

- A company, Erica Fashions, changes its credit and collection policy. This affects those customers who may prefer to buy on credit even if they know that prices are inflated to provide for credit risks (the possibility of bad debts). Some customers may therefore prefer to buy clothes from a store such as Edgars, Milady's, Queenspark or Truworths which offers credit facilities, rather than from Erica Fashions, which does not.

The market environment is also influenced by the macro environment. During a downward trend in the economy, for example, customers have less money to spend on luxury items and this will lead to a reduced sale of luxury products, such as expensive dinner services, clothing and some cars.

Three variables are peculiar to the market environment, namely:

- the market
- the competition
- the suppliers of resources and services.

The market

Here we refer in an abstract sense to 'the market' which concerns the customer and their needs, rather than the physical marketplace.

The business manufactures (or buys) products and may provide services with the idea of selling these to either individual customers or other businesses or institutions. However, before a customer can become active in the market, they must have financial means (money) with which to acquire the available goods and/or services. The customer has to choose between different goods and services because they have limited financial means. It can also happen, however, that although the customer has the necessary financial means, they are not prepared to buy the available goods and services.

IMPORTANT INFORMATION

From the point of view of the business, the market includes all individuals, groups or institutions who have specific needs for goods and services, and who are prepared to use their available financial means to acquire these goods and services.

EXAMPLE 2.4

- The market of a clothing chain such as Edgars, Milady's, Queenspark and Truworths includes all people with a need for clothing who are prepared to spend their money on the articles available. The activities of the business are therefore directed at satisfying the customers' needs.

- The market of South African Airways, kulula.com and FlySafair includes all people who need to travel domestically or internationally, and who have the money to pay for the air ticket. Money is the means with which to satisfy a need (to travel).

- Some manufacturing businesses trade only with wholesalers and retailers and not with the general public. Their market therefore comprises other businesses. For example, you cannot buy a writing pad directly from Sappi: you have to obtain it from a retailer selling stationery such as CNA, PNA or Walton's. The retailer, in turn, has bought the writing pad from a miller such as Croxley, who bought the paper from Sappi.

Here is a further breakdown of different market segments:

- **The consumer market:** This market consists of the end-customers who carry out transactions in order to buy or consume items such as clothing, cars and food.

- **The industrial market:** In this market, goods and services are purchased and used for manufacturing products or providing services to end-customers. As mentioned previously, Croxley buys paper from a paper and pulp business such as Sappi in order to manufacture writing pads, envelopes and cards. Similarly, a kitchen cupboard manufacturer also uses the industrial market when it buys pressed-wood panels from Sappi Novaboard to manufacture its products.
- **The resale market:** In this market, manufactured goods are purchased by businesses with the sole purpose of reselling them to individuals or other businesses at a profit. Pick n Pay, Spar and Checkers, for example, buy canned vegetables and fruit (such as Koo and All Gold) to sell at a profit to its customers.
- **The international market:** Markets operating internationally include foreign customers, manufacturers, retailers and authorities. For example, European traders buy South African fruit on the international market.
- **The government market:** In order to provide services and carry out its functions, government and municipal authorities purchase a range of goods and services, such as:
  - furniture and equipment for use in government schools
  - system(s) to pay salaries to teachers, the police and government officials
  - fire-fighting equipment
  - medical supplies and services.

When discussing the market, we should remember that the customer has certain rights. As an entrepreneur, you should be aware of these rights to keep abreast of your customers' needs. Institutions such as the Consumer Council focus on informing customers of their rights.

The customer has the right to:

- **Be informed:** The customer should receive objective information about the available products and services. The business should not mislead or harm the customer by withholding information about a product. For example, the customer has a right to know the ingredients of canned foods and whether they include colourants or preservatives.
- **Exercise personal choice:** A variety of products and services is available on the market and the customer has the right to decide what to buy. For example, the customer has the right to choose between All Gold and Koo products.
- **Be heard:** The business must be geared towards listening and responding to the customers' complaints and requests. For example, if a customer complains about poor service, the entrepreneur or manager should respond.

- **Be protected:** The customer's safety is important and they should be protected by being informed about possible or likely risks. (The warnings on cigarette packets are the best-known example.)

The competition

Competition between different enterprises has never been greater. Consider the variety of cars available today, as well as the number of dealers who sell them: this is competition. The choice between different products indicates that there is competition in the market.

IMPORTANT INFORMATION

Competition essentially means that each business tries to persuade consumers that its products and services are the best, and that consumers should therefore buy from that particular business.

As an entrepreneur, you must be aware of competitor activity, because it may be a threat to your business. You must be aware of new or improved products on the market. Therefore, it is vitally important to be informed about the competition in the external business environment. You must know who your competitors are; where they are situated (the geographic distribution); the products they offer and the quality of those products; the specific markets they serve and their market share; their financial resources; and their general image in the marketplace.

Over and above the fact that businesses compete with one another's products and services, one can also distinguish between various types of competition:

- **Competition between the needs of consumers:** A person may need to go to a new shopping complex and is prepared to spend a certain amount of money there. The person considers either buying new clothes or having something to eat in the shopping centre. This represents competition for the consumer's limited disposable income.

- **Competition between mechanisms for satisfying needs:** Suppose a person is cold while working at a desk and needs to be warm. The person can insulate the room or buy a heater, a hot water bottle or new warm clothes.

- **Competition between products:** With reference to the previous point, suppose the person decides to buy new warm clothes. A range of garments could satisfy their needs, such as formal clothes (a suit), casual wear (jeans, a jersey or leather jacket) or sportswear (a tracksuit).

- **Competition between different trademarks:** If a person decides to buy a woollen suit, they will have to choose between trademarks such as Daisy Style, Jigsaw Clothing and Rochelle Mawona.

The suppliers of resources and services

Entrepreneurs must decide which products they are going to manufacture and market, the quantities they can produce, and the capital outlay required and affordable for the project. However, the entrepreneur will be dependent on other institutions in the external environment to carry out these activities, because they will not necessarily have the raw materials to manufacture the products. The entrepreneur will, therefore, have to rely on external suppliers for many products or services.

EXAMPLE 2.5

A business that manufactures wooden furniture interacts with the external environment in the following ways:

- To manufacture its furniture the company must buy wood, tools, glue, nails and various other products. All of these must be bought from external suppliers.

- The business uses water, electricity, communication and other services. All of these must be bought from the external environment, such as Eskom for electricity and Telkom for communication services.

- The business must make use of a bank or other financial institution so that it can pay wages, salaries and suppliers. It may also need a loan at some stage, for instance if it wants to expand and build new premises.

- The business decides to build a bigger factory. It must use the services of an external property broker to buy the land and external builders and contractors to build the new premises.

- The larger factory needs additional staff. The business decides to use an external recruitment company to fill the new vacancies.

- Finally, the business must sell its furniture. To do this, they use an intermediary – in this case a wholesaler – who markets the product and sells it to a retailer (for example, Joshua Doore), who then sells the furniture to the end-customer.

2.3.3   The macro environment

The macro environment surrounds the business and its marketing environment. It is made up of a wide range of variables which can affect the business and its marketing activities either positively or negatively.

DEFINITION   The macro environment consists of all the variables and factors outside the business which have a positive or negative influence on the growth and continued existence of the business, and which encourage or hinder the achievement of its objectives.

The individual business has no control over the macro environment or the variables which operate within it. For example, a business has no control over changes in interest or exchange rates. However, these changes affect every business in some way.

The macro environment consists of a number of sub-environments, which are usually described as 'variables' or 'forces'. These include economic, socio-cultural, technological, statutory, physical, political and international influences and forces.

What follows is a brief discussion of each of the sub-environments already identified.

Economic environment (economic conditions)

The economic environment is that part of the macro environment consisting of factors which influence the personal disposable income of the customer as well as their purchasing behaviour. (The term 'customer' is used here in its widest sense; it also includes other businesses.) The customer has limited financial means to satisfy all their needs and is, therefore, forced to make choices.

The customer's disposable income is influenced by many economic factors, for example interest rates and exchange rates, inflation, trade cycles and the economic growth rate.

Interest rates

An interest rate indicates the price at which money can be bought, in other words, the price at which money is available in the money and capital markets. If the interest rate is 20% per annum for a long-term loan of R100 000, this means that the borrower must pay R20 000 per year (20/100 × R100 000) to secure the loan. This is the price which the borrower must pay for the money they wish to borrow.

A rise in interest rates usually depresses spending. If someone wants to buy a car, for example, they will have to pay more to borrow the money and, ultimately, pay more for the car. Suppose the buyer buys a car through hire-purchase financing and the interest rates subsequently rise. This means that the buyer's monthly instalments will rise too and that he or she will pay even more for the vehicle. The bond on a home loan works in the same way: as interest rates rise, so do monthly loan instalments. The opposite is also true.

Inflation

Inflation causes a continual rise in the prices of products and services. This depresses the economy because the purchasing power of the rand, and thus of the customer, decreases as inflation rises. The customer is able to buy fewer products for the same amount of money, because the value of the money has decreased. According to Statistics South Africa and the Reserve Bank, the annual inflation rate in South Africa increased in January 2022 to 5,70% from 3,27% in January 2021, with a quarterly inflation of 1,05% in the 4th quarter of 2021.

EXAMPLE 2.6

In 1980, we paid 30c for a loaf of white bread. Today, we pay R14,50 for the same loaf of bread. In 1980, we paid 76c for a dozen eggs; in 1985, we paid R1,31 and today, we pay R36,00.

Trade cycles

All economies are subject to cyclical change. We can distinguish between different phases in the economic cycle, namely a period of prosperity, followed by a period of recession and depression, and then a period of recovery. As an entrepreneur you should be aware of the phase through which the economy is moving as it influences the management, growth and continued existence of your business. Each phase makes its own demands on the business:

- During a phase of prosperity, the business (the marketing and production divisions) has the opportunity to manufacture and market new products. The business, therefore, can explore new markets and expand its share of the market.

- By contrast, during a recession, customers' disposable incomes are lower and they therefore buy less. This has a direct influence on the demand for products and/or services and therefore the growth of a business.

- According to Statistics South Africa (SAnews.gov.za, 2018), South Africa's worst fears were realised when the country entered the third quarter of 2018 in a technical recession, meaning the country had experienced two quarters of negative economic growth.

Social environment

The social environment is governed by the demographics of the population and social and cultural variables. We can distinguish between the following demographic variables, all of which have an impact on the market:

Size and composition of the population

- **Population growth:** The size and composition of the market are directly influenced by the population growth of the country. When considering the size of the population, remember that families have grown smaller over the past few years, and consider what effect this will have on future markets.

- **Market composition:** The market is made up of different ethnic groups. Each group has a distinctive culture and lifestyle.

- **Changing role of women:** Women make up a large proportion of the labour force today. This has a direct effect on the market, because the needs of a woman who is employed differ from the needs of a woman who is a homemaker. For instance, more working mothers means a greater demand for crèches and nursery schools; families with two incomes have a higher disposable income; the clothing needs of the working woman differ from those of the homemaker; and, finally, working women usually spend more on time-saving goods such as ready-made foods.

- **Life expectancy:** Life expectancy has increased as a result of better medical services and healthier lifestyles. This means that the many citizens over the age of 60 represent marketing opportunities. For example, in the tourist industry there are many opportunities for travel agents to develop tour packages for this target group.

Geographic location

Markets in the metropolitan areas are larger and more concentrated, meaning that a wider variety of products and services can be marketed and sold in and around the cities. Urbanisation and the depopulation of the rural areas have a direct influence on the distribution of the market.

Development level of the market

In South Africa today, great emphasis is being laid on training. Customers are better informed, which means they know precisely what they want and therefore make greater demands on businesses. The customer is aware of, and stands up for, their rights. To continue to exist and grow, every business must focus on the needs of customers.

Other considerations

Social and cultural forces from the macro environment which must be considered include the following:

- **Changing awareness:** The customer today is well informed about quality and available options. They are aware of environmental concerns and take into account whether the manufacturing of products contributes to carbon emissions or uses scarce resources.

- **Time:** In today's busy world, the customer does not want to spend too much time on shopping, and will look for products that are convenient and save time. Some examples include portable laptop computers that can be used while travelling, or prepared foods. A further example is the appearance of convenience supermarkets in residential areas. People returning home from work want to be able to buy essentials as quickly as possible. The convenience and longer opening hours of the smaller supermarkets in suburban areas satisfy this need. The same principle applies to one-stop shopping centres: everything the customer wants is available under one roof.

- **Healthier lifestyle:** The current trend towards fitness and a healthier lifestyle is another force the business must be aware of. There is a greater demand for natural foods (foods without colouring agents or preservatives) and an increased demand for products linked to fitness, such as bicycles, running shoes and gymnasium apparatus.

Technological environment

Technology affects all people in all enterprises and in all industries. It influences the effectiveness, efficiency and productivity of workers. Businesses can now produce their products using fewer resources. The technological environment includes all aspects which give rise to new or improved products and services being made available on the market.

EXAMPLE 2.7

The technological environment embraces numerous aspects that give rise to new products and services being made available on the market. The microwave oven, today a common convenience appliance in the average household, was unknown to previous generations. This product, which is the result of technological development, has given many enterprises the opportunity to develop new products.

If a business does not keep abreast of changes taking place on the technological front, it will soon find that the products it sells are obsolete. The consumer is not interested in obsolete products. Enterprises that do not keep abreast of technological change will have to relinquish their share of the market in the long term. A further influence of the technological environment on the business is that provision should be made for research and development by means of funds allocated for this purpose. Technological changes do not always result in new products – they can also result in improvements to existing products. A good example of this is the cell phone industry.

Physical environment

The physical environment means the natural resources within the country, and incorporates the total management of these resources. Natural resources include gold, coal, diamonds, water and natural forests. The natural beauty of the country can be included here as this influences the tourist market. The following variables in the physical environment should be taken into consideration:

Limited and expensive resources
The world's natural resources are limited and must be managed carefully. Customers today demand that manufacturers recognise these limitations. This could also create opportunities in two ways:

1. the business can advertise its own environmentally friendly procedures and thereby attract customers
2. the business can expand in a new direction, as illustrated in Example 2.8.

EXAMPLE 2.8

- Currently South Africa has problems with the supply of electricity. Many entrepreneurial opportunities have arisen from this area – solar heating for water, power-saving light bulbs and wind generators.

- Water supplies in South Africa are limited, so possible opportunities for entrepreneurs include sprinkler systems using recycled water and toilets with the two-flush option.

Environmentalism and pollution

Industry is often guilty of air, water and noise pollution resulting from their manufacturing processes. The effects of this pollution and the role played by industry in combating pollution are receiving worldwide attention. Manufacturing businesses can play a role by considering issues such as packaging. Packaging in plastic is very convenient, but has definite disadvantages for the environment, so recycling is being widely encouraged. More importantly, some companies are responding by reducing the use of plastics in packaging – or, even better, reducing the total amount of packaging.

Occasionally, poisonous waste products like plastics, which are extremely harmful to human, water and plant life, flow into rivers and the sea. The mining of minerals sometimes elicits strong opposition from conservationists, for example the polemic regarding the mining of minerals in the Limpopo and Mpumalanga provinces and the St Lucia area. The construction of roads can harm the natural scenery; for example, conservationists have strongly opposed the proposed coastal road on the Wild Coast in the Eastern Cape, where pollution from accidents of particularly oil carriers could potentially endanger the delicate ecosystem.

Political and statutory environment

Fiscal and monetary policies of the government of the day influence business. For instance, interest rates have a direct effect on net income, municipal rates affect property tax, and of course the annual budget influences the entire economy. The national budget is a useful document to study because it contains details of likely future spending and how income will be generated from taxes. Variable influences on an individual business include those listed below.

Statutory provisions

Businesses must comply with various statutory provisions. For example, every business must:

- have a trading licence before it can operate

- register as a taxpayer at the local South African Revenue Service (SARS) office

- comply with statutory provisions when concluding contracts
- comply with municipal health requirements, if the business is involved in the food industry.

Two important changes were brought about by the amendments to the Companies Act 71 of 2008, which came into effect on 1 May 2011:

1. The new Consumer Protection Act 68 of 2008 (CPA), which came into effect on 31 March 2011, is being implemented by the National Consumer Commission (NCC), taking over from the Department of Trade and Industry's Office of Consumer Protection (OCP).
2. The Companies and Intellectual Property Commission (CIPC) was established on 1 May 2011. The CIPC will register companies, promote awareness of company and intellectual property law, and monitor compliance of financial reporting standards.

These changes will be discussed in more detail in Chapter 4.

Trade unions

Every business has a responsibility towards its employees. There are various laws which help to maintain a smooth relationship between the employers and employees. In addition to statutory provisions and regulations protecting the rights of the employee, trade unions are an important variable in the macro environment.

The voice of individual employees can easily be ignored by management, therefore trade unions fight for the rights of those workers who are in the same branch of industry. The employee acquires bargaining power through the trade union, which enables them to negotiate, for example, for higher salaries or better working conditions. In other words, the trade union's main function is to negotiate on behalf of its members. Trade unions also defend and advance workers' rights and working conditions. In South Africa there are numerous trade unions, for example, for mine workers, the motor industry, the steel industry and bank officials. If disputes are not resolved or are unfairly resolved, the Labour Relations Act 66 of 1995 has made it possible to refer these cases to external mechanisms, such as the Commission for Conciliation, Mediation and Arbitration (CCMA).

Associations and institutes

Many business associations and institutes exist to advance the interests of businesses in their fields in the same way that trade unions act in the interests of organised labour. Earlier on in this chapter, we emphasised that a business has little – if any – influence over the macro environment. By means of associations and institutes, a business can promote its interests in its industry by collaborating with other businesses in its industry.

The following institutes and associations are well known and active in the macro environment:

- Afrikaanse Handelsinstituut (AHI)
- The South African Chamber of Business (Sacob)
- The Chamber of Mines
- The Motor Industries Federation
- Black Management Forum.

International environment

The variables influencing individual businesses originate from the local sphere (the business itself) and the national sphere (the market and macro environments). Over and above all these forces, the business must also still keep abreast of variables operating in the international sphere. These influences originate in the environment outside the country's borders and include the following:

International technology

In certain areas such as synthetic fuels, mining and veterinary science, South Africa is technologically developed. However, like all developing countries, South Africa also imports technology, such as computer technology from the USA and engineering technology from Germany and Japan. This is a phenomenon common to all developing countries.

International politics

South Africa felt the effect of international politics with the trade sanctions imposed in the mid-1980s. The country did not have access to foreign loan capital, for example, and this had a negative effect on the economic growth rate and job creation. In a tweet President Trump of the USA asked the US Secretary of State to investigate into the reports of land seizures without compensation as a means to achieve equality and racial justice. This remark raised concern that the US could punish South Africa economically. Now, South Africa is the biggest beneficiary of the African Growth and Opportunity Act, which grants many of its products duty-free access to US markets.

International economy

Economic factors and variables such as interest rates, exchange rates, the gold price, the economic growth rate, inflation, the availability of capital and a scarcity of resources occur worldwide and influence the economic conditions of all countries. For example, think of the effect inflation has had on the economies of Zimbabwe, Russia and Argentina. Among other things, high inflation rates resulted in very high food prices in these countries.

2.4 Summary

The rand–US dollar and other exchange rates significantly influence South African import and export activities. If the rand–dollar exchange rate is weak, the cost of importing goods becomes higher for a South African business. For example, imported textbooks are currently expensive because the rand–dollar (or sterling) exchange rate is unfavourable for South African booksellers.

A business cannot function in total isolation. Without interaction with the business environment, achieving your objectives will remain a dream and your business will not continue to grow, and may even cease to exist.

A business is an independent body that is established by an entrepreneur to provide products or services that will meet the needs of consumers, and consists of all the business functions. An establishment is the place where inputs are converted into outputs. This is the place where the physical production takes place, in other words the factory or plant.

Businesses are classified into five sectors, according to the activities that they perform:

- **Primary sector:** Exploitation of natural resources in their raw unprocessed form.
- **Secondary sector:** Natural resources processed into final products.
- **Tertiary sector:** Responsible for conveying or distributing final products from the manufacturer to the consumer.
- **Quaternary sector:** Comprises intellectual activities often associated with technological innovation, sometimes called the knowledge economy.
- **Quinary sector:** Includes the highest levels of decision-making in a society or economy.

However, if we look at the route that an individual product follows from its original stage until it ends up in the hands of the consumer, we combine the sectors in an industrial column.

The business environment can positively or negatively affect the business and, therefore, the entrepreneur must be aware of the variables in the business environment. The business environment consists of the external environment (macro and market environments), which is the environment outside the business that affects the growth and existence of the business, and the internal environment, which is the business itself and is generally described as the micro environment. The different components of the business environment, as identified are not independent of one another, but there is a constant interaction between them.

The entrepreneur must continually gather information as a basis for analysing market trends. This information must be transformed into knowledge to bridge the gap between the enterprise, the entrepreneur and the market. From this knowledge, the entrepreneur can analyse potential opportunities and threats.

The business environment offers opportunities which help the entrepreneur achieve the objectives of the business. Conversely, if the entrepreneur does not attend to important signals in the business environment, this could jeopardise the business.

SELF-EVALUATION QUESTIONS

1. Multiple choice questions

    (a) The strategy, goals and business capabilities are part of the … environment.

       (i)   macro   (ii)   market

       (iii) mega   (iv) micro

    (b) Technology can be seen as:

       (i)   a regulatory factor   (ii)   an uncontrollable factor

       (iii) a controllable factor   (iv) an environmental variable

    (c) New and better products and procedures refer to the … environment.

       (i)   market   (ii)   economic

       (iii) consumer's   (iv) technological

    (d) Critical variables such as consumerism, division of income and language division are part of the … environment.

       (i)   economic   (ii)   social

       (iii) cultural   (iv) consumer's

    (e) The availability, conservation and utilisation of resources are part of:

       (i)   the physical environment

       (ii) government policy

       (iii) consumerism

       (iv) the social environment

2. With the aid of a practical example, illustrate the relationship between the business and the establishment.

3. Discuss the five sectors in which businesses and establishments can be grouped and substantiate your discussion with practical examples.

4. Draw your own industrial column for the production of wine.

5. Explain the meaning of the concept 'business environment' and, drawing on your experience, identify its most important characteristics.

6. Give reasons why a business cannot exist in total isolation and continue to grow.

7. Name three components of the business environment and give a description of each.

8. Discuss the micro environment and its variables.

9. Identify the variables in the market environment and discuss each one.

10. With the help of examples, discuss the different markets in which a business that is manufacturing wooden furniture can conduct business transactions.

11. Identify your rights as a customer and illustrate each right with a practical example.

12. Clarify the meaning of 'competition'. Illustrate your answer with practical examples.

13. Do you think it is necessary for the business to take the macro environment into account? Give reasons for your answer by discussing the different variables within the sub-environments.

14. Suppose you are the owner of a business that manufactures and markets wooden kitchen cupboards. Evaluate your business environment on the basis of the variables in the micro, macro and market environments.

15. Vusi owns a business which sells computer equipment. He realises that he must take the variables in the external environment into account. However, he focuses only on the variables in the market environment and does not consider those in the macro environment. Explain to Vusi, with the help of suitable examples, which variables can be identified in the macro environment and what influence these may have on his business.

REFERENCES AND FURTHER READING

Bateman, TS & Snell, AS. 2002. *Management Leading & Collaborating in a Competitive World*. New York: McGraw-Hill.

Certo, SC & Certo, ST. 2014. *Modern Management Concepts and Skills*. Boston: Pearson.

Daft, RL. 2012. *New Era of Management*. Mason, Ohio: South-Western Cengage Learning.

De Beer, AA & Rossouw, D. 2015. *Focus on Operational Management: A Generic Approach,* 3rd edition. Cape Town: Juta.

Hellriegel, D, Jackson, SE, Slocum, J, Staude, G, Amos, T, Klopper, HB, Louw, L & Oosthuizen, T. 2004. *Management*. Cape Town: Oxford University Press.

Nel, J & De Beer, A. 2014. *Business Management: A Contemporary Approach*. Cape Town: Juta.

Nieuwenhuizen, C. (ed). 2014. *Basics of Entrepreneurship*, 3rd edition. Cape Town: Juta.

Palmer, A & Hartley, B. 2009. *The Business Environment*. London: McGraw-Hill.

SAnews.gov.za. 2018. SA exits technical recession in third quarter. 2018. https://www.sanews.gov.za/south-africa/sa-exits-technical-recession-third-quarter#:~:text=South%20Africa%20has%20come%20out%20of%20a%20technical,by%202.2%25%20in%20the%20third%20quarter%20of%202018 (Accessed 28 September 2022).

Van Noordwyk, A, Fernandes, NMJ & Van Zyl, JH. (eds). 2015. *Business Functions: An Introduction*, 2nd edition. Cape Town: Juta.

Williams, C. 2013. *Principles of Management*, 7th edition. Canada: South-Western.

Legislation

Companies Act 71 of 2008.

Consumer Protection Act 68 of 2008.

Labour Relations Act 66 of 1995.

THE IDENTIFICATION AND DEVELOPMENT OF BUSINESS IDEAS

HANNELIZE JACOBS

LEARNING OUTCOMES

After you have studied this chapter, you should be able to:

- LO 1: Implement the stages of setting up a business
- LO 2: Cultivate a creative attitude
- LO 3: Generate business ideas
- LO 4: Develop and evaluate business ideas

Introduction

Whether you are already running a successful business, or you have just started thinking about becoming your own boss, every entrepreneur shares a common responsibility: developing new products that customers find attractive and keeping the business running. However, doing so is much easier said than done. One of the most important elements of the decision-making process on a business start-up is the identification and evaluation of business opportunities. Throughout the world, there are millions of entrepreneurs with testimonies suggesting that there are numerous potential sources of new viable business ideas. The purpose of this chapter is the identification and development of business ideas. The first part of the chapter will look at the three stages of setting up a business. After that, we will define the term 'creativity' and look at how you can determine your own level of creativity as well as how you can increase your own creative thinking. After this discussion, we will consider all the techniques for the generation of business ideas. Lastly, we will focus on the development and evaluation of business ideas to be able to convert them into a business enterprise.

LO 1: Implement the stages of setting up a business

3.1 Setting up a business

Setting up a business can be divided into three main stages, namely:

1. identifying a feasible and viable business idea (the idea stage)
2. drawing up a business plan (the planning stage)
3. implementing the business plan (the implementation stage).

Figure 3.1 illustrates the three-stage process that is the theme of the rest of the book. In this chapter, the first stage will be discussed: the identification and development of business ideas. Chapters 4 and 5 deal with the planning stage, and Chapter 6 discusses the implementation stage.

Identifying business ideas is a creative process. A prospective entrepreneur must, therefore, be able to cultivate a creative attitude. Everyone has the potential to think creatively. In this chapter, certain techniques will be introduced that can be used to improve the creative mindset of an entrepreneur. Although it is important to think of as many business ideas as possible, only one idea can eventually be converted into a business enterprise. This chapter will assist in identifying a suitable idea (ie a feasible and viable business idea).

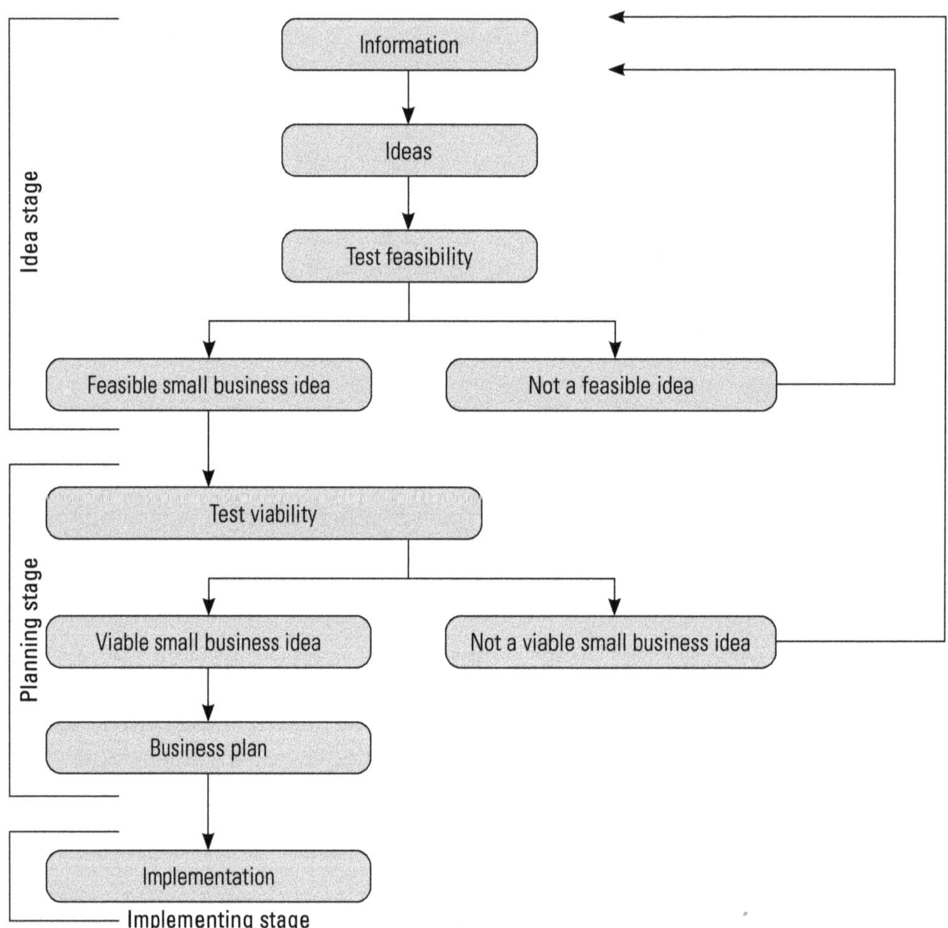

FIGURE 3.1: The three stages of setting up a business

Example 3.1 is an example of a feasible business idea.

EXAMPLE 3.1

Maggie's Mobile Pet Grooming Service

Maggie Phillips worked as an administrative manager for the Pierre van Ryneveld Veterinary Clinic for four years. Over these four years, she heard many owners complain that they do not have the time to give their dogs a bath themselves, or to take them to a dog parlour. Maggie thought that the dogs and their owners would appreciate the convenience of a mobile pet grooming service. After Maggie determined that there was no immediate competition in the surrounding area, she resigned and started her own enterprise, *Maggie's Mobile Pet Grooming Service*.

Maggie started on a small scale, since she did not have much capital. She used her savings to buy shampoos, conditioners, grooming tools, towels, clippers and dryers, and a grooming table. She had to take out a loan of R100 000, which she would have to pay back over a period of three years, to purchase a fully equipped truck with a small geyser. Maggie employed one of her friends, Sarah, to help her handle the dogs during the grooming process.

Maggie's Mobile Pet Grooming Service initially offered one package, a Standard Grooming Package, which included a wash and rinse with shampoo and warm water, towel dry, styling brush out, and a hair accessory. Her prices were determined according to the size of the dog. Some of their clients had specific dog breeds that not only needed the usual wash and dry, but also a cut and styling. Sarah identified this opportunity and suggested that they offer a second package, a styling package, which included the standard package as well as clipping and scissor styling (breed-specific cuts) and teeth cleaning.

Maggie did not advertise her mobile pet grooming services and relied on her friends and her former work colleagues at the veterinary clinic to tell other people about her services. To render a service on an order basis requires extremely good planning, as well as excellent administration. Since Maggie had worked as an administrative manager, Maggie and Sarah decided that Maggie should be responsible for the general management and the information management functions. Philippa was appointed as administrative assistant to help Maggie answer the telephone, take orders, send out accounts, keep records and file documents.

LO 2: Cultivate a creative attitude

3.2 Cultivating an entrepreneur's creative attitude

Chapter 1 explained that the capacity to act creatively and innovatively is one of the characteristics of an entrepreneur. Although a new and innovative business idea can be satisfying, it may be very difficult to establish – it is not always easy to be the first to come up with a new product or service. Being first, you have to convince others that there is a need for your product or service. And being second or third means having to learn from the mistakes of others.

This does not, however, imply that others' ideas should be imitated and offered to the market. An entrepreneur should try to provide specialised or unique products or services. Think of an idea or ideas that will distinguish your business from a competitor's business. To do this, you must think and act creatively.

Entrepreneurship is not an easy career path – it is rather complex. There are many qualities that can help individuals in the process of becoming an entrepreneur, such as commitment and determination (as discussed in Chapter 1). However, one characteristic is more valuable than all the other characteristics, namely creativity (Barnes, 2017).

3.2.1   What is creativity?

DEFINITION   Creativity is commonly defined as the generation of novel and useful ideas. Being creative is generating a variety of really different ideas. According to Franken (1993:396), a more descriptive definition of creativity is the tendency to generate or recognise ideas, alternatives or possibilities that may be useful in solving problems, communicating with others, and entertaining ourselves and others.

Creativity involves first, novelty or originality – for example, creative ideas should either recombine or completely change existing elements – and second, usefulness or appropriateness – for example, creative ideas should be suitable for the work task or the imminent problem (George, 2007:439; Amabile & Mueller, 2008).

In order to be creative, you should be able to view things in new ways or from fresh perspectives. Among other things, you must be able to generate new possibilities or new alternatives. Being creative is not only about the number of alternatives that can be generated, but about the uniqueness of these ideas.

3.2.2   Am I creative?

How do you recognise creativity? Think of half a dozen people you believe to be creative. They could include those around you or perhaps famous South African inventors, such as Mark Shuttleworth, who invented an electronic security system, and Chris Barnard, who developed surgical procedures for organ transplants, invented new heart valves and performed the first human heart transplant, or Allan Cormack, a South African physicist who together with British electrical engineer Godfrey Hounsfield invented the CAT scan, which secured them the 1979 Nobel Prize in Medicine (Cormack & Hounsfield, 1979).

The Covid-19 pandemic has propelled numerous inventions globally. Michael Lucas, a South African invented antimicrobial surface coatings that make surfaces capable of self-sanitising. By applying it to existing surfaces, such as common hospital surfaces, it reduces the risk of infections, saving not only money for the government and hospitals but also lives. Engineers from Mercedes, the German automotive brand, together with engineers and clinicians at University College London, have come up with a breathing aid that reduces the need for ventilators and could be mass-produced quickly. The device, called the CPAP (continuous positive airway pressure), has in trials in hospitals in Italy and China reduced the need for ventilators by about 50%.

Which characteristics or abilities do these people have in common that make them creative? The obvious abilities may include:

- solving problems in a different way
- seeing possibilities others have not seen
- thinking imaginatively
- initiating change.

The creative person usually enjoys problem-solving and tends to bring fresh perspectives to old problems. Example 3.2 provides some fun problems to stimulate creativity.

EXAMPLE 3.2

- You are participating in a race. You overtake the second person. Which position are you in?

Answer: If you answered that you are first, then you are absolutely wrong! If you overtake the second person and you take his place, you are second!

- If you overtake the last person, then where in the race would you be?

Answer: If you answered that you are second to last, then you are wrong again. It would not be possible to overtake the last person!

- If a red house is made of red bricks, and a blue house is made of blue bricks, what is a greenhouse made of?

Answer: If you answered that a greenhouse is made of green bricks, you are wrong. A greenhouse is made of glass.

- Draw four straight lines which go through the middle of all of the dots without taking the pencil off the paper.

Answer:

- There are six eggs in a basket. Six people each take one of the eggs. How can it be that one egg is left in the basket?

Answer:

The last person took the basket with the last egg still inside.

Creative thought can be divided into divergent and convergent reasoning.

DEFINITION   Divergent thinking is the intellectual ability to think of many original, diverse and elaborate ideas.

Convergent thinking is the intellectual ability to evaluate, critique and choose logically the best idea from a selection of ideas.

Divergent and convergent reasoning are both necessary for creative output. Divergent thinking, also referred to as lateral thinking, is a thought process used to generate ideas by exploring many possible solutions related to a problem, such as brainstorming. On the other hand, convergent thinking is a thought process used to organise and structure the many solutions to arrive at a single best solution to a problem, such as a multiple choice test.

Research has shown that divergent (creative) thinking is natural for right-brain dominant people, whereas convergent (logical) thinking is natural for left-brain dominant people. The right brain processes data in a rapid, complex, whole-pattern and perceptual manner, while the left brain operates in a more verbal, analytic mode.

Brain hemispheric dominance can therefore be an indication of creative ability. Try to test your brain dominance with one or more of the online brain dominance tests at, for example, http://braintest.sommer-sommer.com/en/

Although some are born with the gift of creativity, it is possible for everyone to develop and improve their creative abilities. It is important to understand that creativity is just as much an attitude as a manner of thinking. It is thus possible to think of new ideas by adapting yourself to creativity. The following methods can be used to improve creativity:

- **Actively seek ideas:** You can learn to seek ideas actively by judging everything you read or observe in terms of the ideas that can be developed from it. If you think in this way regularly, it will become a habit and ideas will come more easily.

- **Write your ideas down:** Make a habit of writing down an idea as soon as you have one, even if you feel it is not a good idea. Read through the ideas regularly. Review them and perhaps combine them in a new concept.

- **View a topic from another person's perspective:** Put yourself in somebody else's position to get a different view of a topic. With a better understanding of others' points of view, you will gain new insights and ideas. By asking yourself, for example, what the mother of a pre-school child thinks of the concept 'to see red', and then looking at the same idea from the perspective of a busy businesswoman or a widowed grandmother, you can generate entirely new ideas.

- **Break your routine:** A good way of stimulating your thoughts is to break your routine. Here are a few suggestions:
  - Note how you perform everyday actions, such as washing dishes, and then do them differently.
  - Spend a whole day without something that is a part of a daily routine, for example your cell phone.
  - Browse the web on a subject that you know nothing about.
  - Start a conversation with a stranger or someone you would not normally speak to.
  - Do something you have never done before, such as going to the theatre, riding a horse or starting a new hobby or sport. In other words, broaden your horizons.

- **Explore the grey areas:** If you tend to see only the right and wrong sides of a case, it is time to explore the grey areas between right and wrong. Make a habit of looking for different solutions and possibilities. Start by completing the following incomplete questions. See how many solutions you can find to each in ten minutes:
  - What will happen if I ...?
  - In what different way can I ... ?
  - Who will benefit by ... ?

- **Use a creative technique:** Use formal techniques such as Bob Eberle's S.C.A.M.P.E.R. Each letter of the acronym represents a different way you can play with new ideas (Mansfield, 2018):
    - **Substitute:** What happens if we switch two things around?
    - **Combine:** What if we add these two things together?
    - **Adapt:** Is there another use? Can we invent one?
    - **Modify:** What can you emphasise, hide or change?
    - **Put to Other Uses:** A brick can be a paperweight. A shoe can be a doorstop.
    - **Eliminate:** What can we delete – and what does that do?
    - **Rearrange (or Reverse):** Why not turn it upside down?

Before you start looking for business ideas, take some time to adjust your mind to creativity. This mindset will eventually help you to identify new or better business ideas.

3.2.3 Team creativity

There are at least 200 different techniques and tools to enhance the creativity of teams, for example:

- Brain sketching
- Brainstorming
- Bunches of bananas
- Card storyboards
- Creative problem-solving (CPS)
- Idea advocate
- Pin cards
- Superheroes
- Trigger sessions
- Visualising goals
- Rotating roles
- Storyboarding
- Forced connections
- Brain-writing
- SCAMPER
- Wishing
- Questioning assumptions
- Six thinking hats®

Some of the tools and techniques listed above are discussed below:

Brain sketching

Brain sketching involves passing evolving sketches around a group. Limited facilitation skills are required. Brain sketching is typically conducted in the following manner:

- A group of between four and eight people sit around a table or in a circle. They need to be far enough apart to have some privacy. The problem statement is agreed to and discussed until it is understood.

- Each participant privately draws one or more sketches (each on separate sheets of paper) of how the problem might be solved, passing each sketch on to the person on their right when it is finished. The facilitator suggests that sketches should not take more than five minutes to draw.
- Participants take the sketches passed to them and either develop or annotate them or use them to stimulate new sketches of their own, passing the amended original and/or any new sketches on to their neighbour on the right when ready.
- After the process has been running for a suitable period or energy is running down, the sketches can be collected.
- It will probably help to display all the sketches and discuss them in turn for clarification and comments.
- The team then moves on to a categorisation, evaluation and selection process.

Pin cards

- There are between five and eight members in a group.
- Each team member gets a few index cards. The problem is written on a visible board (Markov, 2018).
- Each team member writes one idea on a card and puts it on their right side.
- When team members run out of ideas, they choose a card from the pile on their left and try to add to it. If they cannot, they shift it to the pile on their right and get another card. If they can add to the idea, they write it on a new card, attach the two cards together, and move both to the pile on the right.
- The moderator should keep the cards circulating.
- The process is completed at the end of a predetermined time (eg 30 minutes).

Superheroes

Superheroes is a fantasy-based technique. Participants pretend to be a fictional (or real) superhero (like Superman, The Incredible Hulk, Batman, James Bond, Wonder Woman, Sherlock Holmes or Spiderman) and use their 'superpowers' to trigger ideas.

This technique is good for creating an atmosphere of light-hearted fun in which energy is high and fantasy and metaphor acceptable. All superheroes have skills and capacities that are outside 'normal' life. This means that people tend to think outside of the norm and that they play a role that allows them to express more unusual ideas than they might normally.

Superhero stories also have strong elements of wish-fulfilment and can therefore help people to express wishes. The stories may not be suitable for serious or introverted groups, or groups without a level of trust. Here is how you can facilitate this technique:

- Prepare some general information on each superhero. This might include their name, special powers, weaknesses, background and a picture. You can also provide props if you have an extrovert in the group.

- Display and discuss the problem to ensure everyone understands the issue. It can be useful to brainstorm in order to list the more obvious ideas. (Brainstorming is a technique to build on others' ideas. Members of the group put forward ideas without interruption or evaluation from the others.)

- Select a superhero for each participant. (Each could also choose one for themselves or take one from the facilitator's information pack.) Give them time to think a little about that superhero and talk to them about what life is like as a superhero in order to help them get into the role.

- The superhero characters are then used as the basis of an excursion. The extrovert groups will get into the role – 'I will heat the chemicals instantly with my laser eyes while freezing the container with my breath' – whereas the more introverted groups will tend to be happier talking in the third person ('Superman could heat the chemicals with his laser eyes . . .').

- Start by getting each superhero to voice a few ideas.

- Allow the group members to trigger off each other's ideas. Perhaps if Superman and Wonder Woman worked together, they could produce an improved solution?

- When you have sufficient ideas, evaluate them.

Trigger sessions

Trigger sessions are a good way of getting lots of ideas from untrained resources and are carried out as follows:

- The person with the problem explains and defines it.

- Each member of the group writes down their ideas quickly (two minutes only).

- One member reads out their list – others silently cross out ideas that are read out and write down ideas that are 'hitch-hiked' (ie triggered by ideas that have been read out).

- The second member reads out their list of ideas not covered on anyone else's list, followed in turn by other members.

- The last member reads out their original list plus their 'hitch-hiked' list. The procedure is then repeated, reversing the original order (for example, if there are six members, the order is: member 1, 2, 3, 4, 5, 6, then 5, 4, 3, 2, 1, then 2, 3, 4, 5, 6 and so on).

A good group will be able to manage several passes. Everyone's paper is then collected and can be typed up into a single list of ideas – all duplicates should have been crossed out during the session.

LO 3: Generate business ideas

3.3 Generating business ideas

A good business idea seldom comes out of the blue or as an inspiration. A potential entrepreneur must look deliberately and think creatively about ideas that can be transformed into a business.

In your search for ideas you can make use of certain structured techniques. The techniques for the generation of business ideas proposed in this book can be divided into five broad approaches, as illustrated in Figure 3.2:

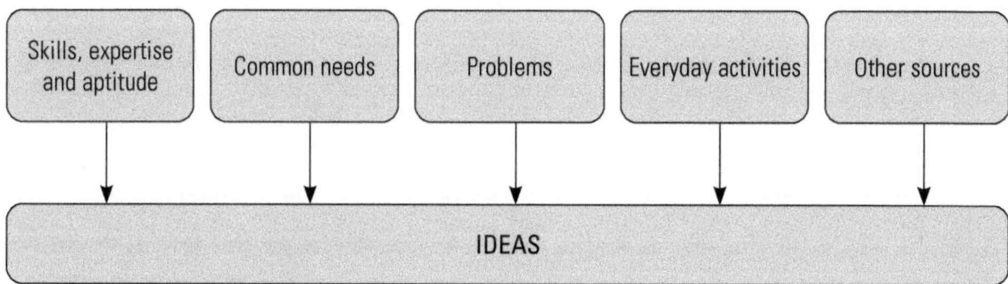

FIGURE 3.2: Generating business ideas

These approaches have been tested successfully and promise to produce positive results and will be discussed in the sections that follow.

3.3.1 The generation of ideas from the entrepreneur's skills, expertise and aptitude

These approaches have been tested successfully and promise to produce positive results and will be discussed in the sections that follow.

Everyone has certain skills. An entrepreneur's skills, expertise and aptitudes are among key factors for success, as discussed in Chapter 1.

In addition to these key factors, consider the following:

* Formal training does not necessarily guarantee success in a business enterprise. This does not mean that your qualifications are useless: through your studies, you can obtain certain knowledge that can lead to a business idea. A tourism student, for example, has gained certain knowledge which could give them the idea and ability to start a unique travel business.

- Skills can also be gained from working experience. As an employee, you are responsible for certain activities. Your knowledge of them can enable you to start a business of your own involving these activities. For example, the fact that you worked as a domestic worker can be the reason why you want to start a cleaning service business.

- Have you developed any skills through your hobbies or other non-career activities that could be used as ideas to start your own business? For example, the fact that you like to work in the garden and have 'green fingers' also now knowing where to plant what, means you have learnt certain gardening skills.

IMPORTANT INFORMATION

- Draw up a profile of your own abilities. List your skills. For example, can you weld or knit? Identify your expertise.

- List your formal qualifications (eg diplomas or certificates) and experience gained (eg handling difficult customers).

- Write down your natural aptitudes or talents and interests. For example, you may be able to communicate well (this is an aptitude). Your interests may be woodwork or building websites.

This list of skills, expertise and aptitudes can now be used to identify business ideas. To show you how this can be done, consider the following example:

EXAMPLE 3.3

Juliet Dhlamini has an eye for a beautiful photograph and works magic with a camera. With these skills, she can provide a product or service to individuals or organisations.

You can identify many business ideas by thinking of how to provide products or services to individuals or organisations, and what types of products or services they might need.

Looking at Example 3.4, you can see how many ideas Juliet, with her single skill, could identify. Now take one of your skills and do a similar exercise.

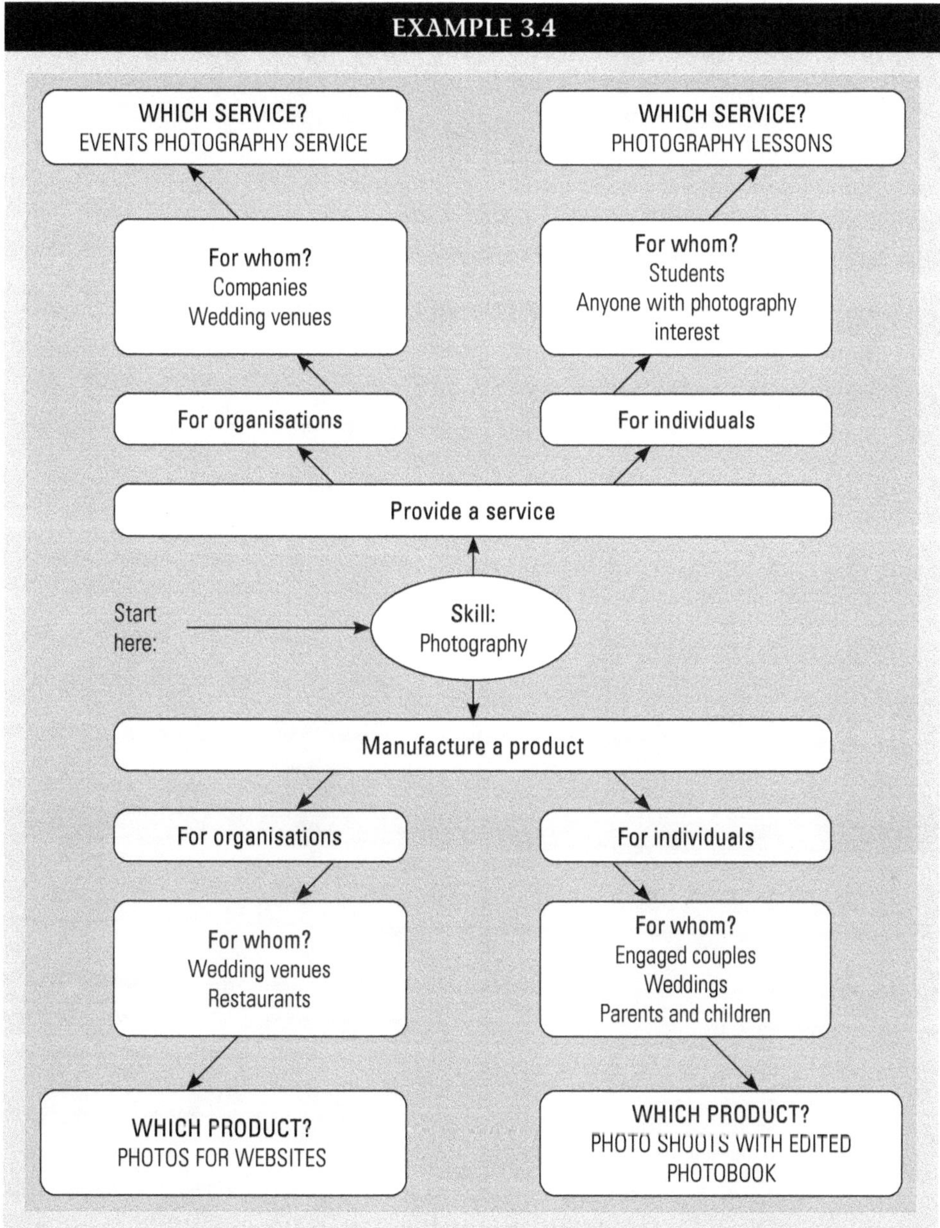

3.3.2   Generating ideas from common needs

Everyone has needs. However, not everyone's needs are the same. The business idea should satisfy a need among a range of people for the same product or service. In other words, the entrepreneur must try to satisfy a common or shared need. Individuals with common needs can usually be grouped together, for example all mothers with small children, all members of a soccer team and all prospective homeowners. You can also identify groups of organisations that have the same need, for example businesses that need catering on a regular basis or businesses that need a complete maintenance service. Think of examples of interest groups and their needs and write them down.

By concentrating on the needs of only one interest group, you will find that many business ideas will cross your mind. Example 3.5 illustrates a technique for generating business ideas from the needs that groups experience – in this case the needs of cyclists.

EXAMPLE 3.5

Suppose we regard cyclists as a group, those who ride bicycles for recreation. Write down the group's needs as you answer the questions in the diagram.

You can use the answers to develop new business ideas.

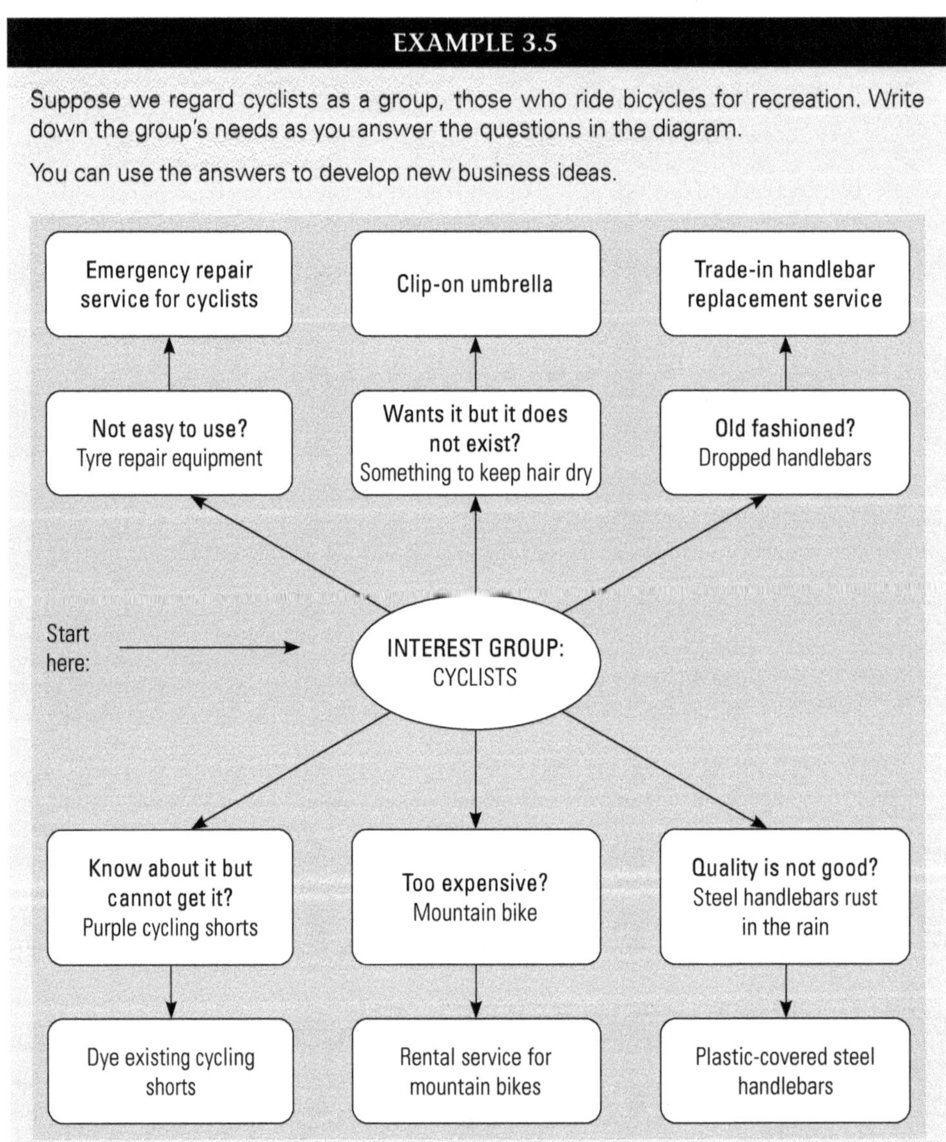

3.3.3 Generating ideas from existing problems

Instead of thinking of unfulfilled needs, you can think of existing, unsolved problems. Think of things that irritate you. Now think of ways of removing those irritations.

EXAMPLE 3.6

Small businesses frequently struggle to keep up with larger businesses, specifically pertaining to infrastructure and human resources tools. The solution to this problem is the 2011-launched ZenPayroll, now called Gusto, which aids small businesses by supplying an easy and affordable way to manage all the payroll-processing aspects, from calculating tax to making payments and direct deposits. It is no wonder that Gusto is changing the world of software solutions for small businesses (Farrell, 2020).

Knowing these problems enables the prospective entrepreneur to find the initial idea for a business that is based on the solution of a specific problem.

Example 3.7 illustrates a technique developed for generating business ideas from everyday problems. This example uses the general problem of traffic jams to illustrate the technique.

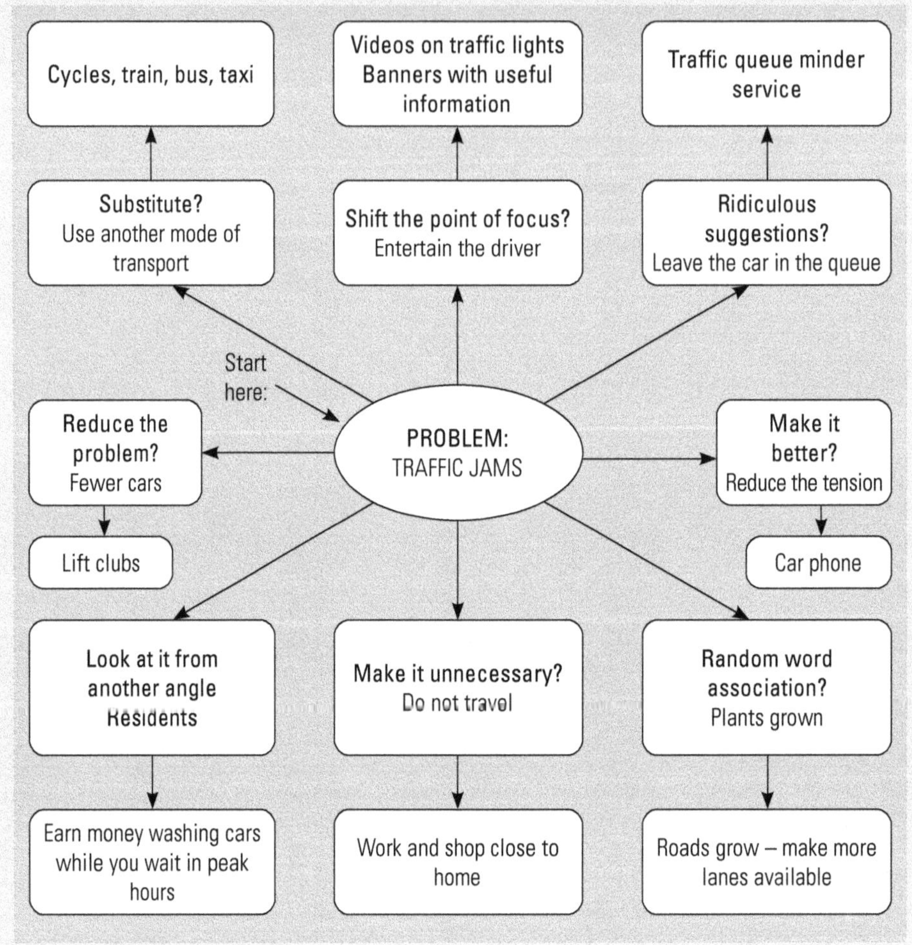

3.3.4 Generating ideas from everyday activities

Many business ideas can be identified merely by awareness of everyday activities. The entrepreneur can use the following methods to identify new business ideas:

- **Use print or electronic media:** Think of products that are advertised on television, in magazines and in newspapers. Ask yourself whether they could be improved, distributed or marketed differently.

- **Look in other places:** Come up with business ideas by looking in unlikely places. The following questions may help:
  - What ideas can you get at an airport, a movie theatre or a church?
  - What ideas can you bring back from a sports meeting, a funfair or a doctor's consulting room?
- **Explore your surroundings:** Explore a part of your city or town that you have not seen before. What do you notice?
- **Observe other cultures:** Take note of the novelties and different ways of doing things at places where you go on holiday.
- **Talk to other people:** Have conversations with your family, friends, colleagues and businesspeople and find out if they have come across possible business ideas. The problem of obtaining holiday accommodation at short notice could, for example, lead to an enterprise that specialises in finding and allocating unused and cancelled holiday accommodation.
- **At work:** Ask yourself if the products and services at your place of work could be improved upon.
- **Go shopping:** Examine some of the products on your next visit to the shops. Remember that no product or service is perfect. By asking questions about the products, new ideas can emerge. Here are some questions to ask yourself:
  - What problems are there with this product?
  - Could the product be improved in any way?
  - Is there a better way for the product to be packaged?
  - Can any new product be added to the present range of products?
  - Can the product be aimed at another market?

EXAMPLE 3.8

The child-lock, which is used on cars to prevent children from opening the door while the vehicle is in motion, is one business idea. Another business idea resulting from everyday activities is renting out expensive hardware tools and venue equipment such as cutlery, crockery, tables and chairs.

- **Changes in your immediate area:** By noting changes or important events that take place around you, new business ideas can be identified.

EXAMPLE 3.9

The crime rate in your neighbourhood is on the increase. This creates an opportunity for an entrepreneur to start a security company for that specific area, putting up booms and patrolling the surrounds.

3.3.5 Generating ideas from other sources

Apart from taking note of everyday activities, ideas can also be found by consulting other reference sources. Figure 3.3 summarises some examples:

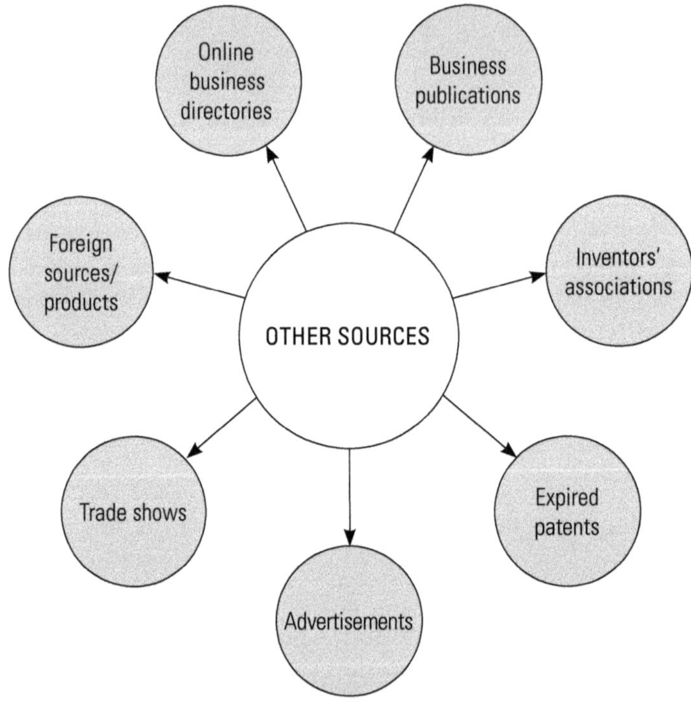

FIGURE 3.3: Other sources to generate ideas from

- **Online business directories:** In the digital age, searching online for business ideas based on what products and services are already on offer is a fitting option. Accessing detailed information, and even online reviews, is possible. Some of the free business directories in South Africa are Hotfrog, Entrepo, Activeweb, Cylex Business Directory, Yellosa, Citylist, Rateitall, FoxList and Snupit.

- **Consult business publications:** Magazines such as WealthWise and SA Franchise Warehouse can be valuable sources of ideas. Entrepreneur Magazine carries up-to-date success stories on successful entrepreneurs in South Africa.

- **Contact an inventors' association:** This can be a rich source of ideas. For example, you might be able to collaborate with an inventor to produce and market their invention. An association that might be useful to contact is the Institute of Inventors and Innovators.

- **Examine patents that have expired:** Expired patents are public property. There can be various reasons why a patent has not been exploited, and it may now be ready for the market. These reasons could include:
  - bigger markets for the product have arisen in the interim
  - the product can now be used with other products that were previously unavailable
  - the product can be manufactured using new technology, which now makes it technically feasible and commercially viable
  - a new use for the product has arisen.

  An example of an expired patent is antibiotics and pills to alleviate muscular injuries. Lennon sells a product called Panamor that is comparable to the well-known product Voltaren. Panamor originated on the expiry of a patent on the original product.

- **Investigate advertisements for business opportunities:** Business opportunities are widely advertised online and in local publications. Although many of these must be investigated with caution, there are real opportunities that can serve as sources of new business ideas. Note, for example, how many franchising opportunities are advertised in the newspapers.

- **Visit trade shows:** Trade shows in a face-to-face, virtual or hybrid format are a good source of ideas. You also get the opportunity to see the physical product and to talk to the exhibitors about the potential market, product features, new technology and even the possibility of doing business together. Examples of face-to-face trade shows are the annual Design Indaba in Cape Town, the Grand Designs Live show in Johannesburg, the My Business Expo Durban, and the Small Business Expo in Johannesburg.

- **Examine overseas products:** Products that are not yet available in South Africa are often imported, imitated or adapted for the South African market. Chicken Licken is an example of a South African business that originated from a business idea obtained abroad, and which has been developed into the biggest fried chicken franchised brand outside the USA.

LO 4: Develop and evaluate business ideas

3.4 Developing and evaluating business ideas

In the previous section, you were encouraged not to limit your creativity but to think about all possible business ideas. However, most of these ideas will not work. The initial sifting of ideas (the convergent reasoning part of creativity) is performed by relying on your personal judgement and intuition.

Only one of the ideas can be chosen and converted into a business on its own or in combination with one or more of the other ideas on the list. To choose the correct business idea, the potential entrepreneur must evaluate each idea on the list.

Although there are examples of entrepreneurs who have converted an idea into a successful business opportunity merely on the strength of intuition, this is not the best way. (Henry Ford, the creator of the Model T Ford, is the exception: he followed his intuition and made millions from it (The Henry Ford, 2022)).

Business ideas can be evaluated primarily by two methods, namely a feasibility study and a viability study.

DEFINITION A feasibility study is a general examination of the potential of the idea to be converted into a business enterprise. This study focuses largely on the ability of the entrepreneur to convert the idea into a business enterprise.

A viability study is an in-depth investigation into the profitability of the idea which is to be converted into a business enterprise.

Before evaluating the ideas, you should first be clear about what each of these ideas suggests. In particular, two things must be clear:

1. What will the main activities of the business be?
2. Who will the customers be?

The activities of the business will consist of two or more of the following:

1. the manufacture of a product
2. the provision of a service
3. the sale of other people's products and/or services.

Your customers will consist of:

- individuals and/or
- organisations.

The 'bow-tie' diagram in Figure 3.4 illustrates these elements:

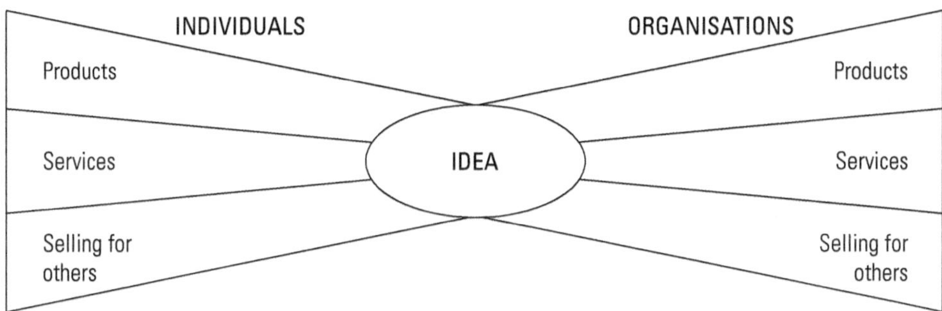

FIGURE 3.4: Bow-tie diagram

The diagram above provides six options for your business, namely:
1. The manufacture of products for individuals
2. Providing services for individuals
3. The sale of other people's products and/or services to individuals
4. The manufacture of products for organisations
5. Providing services for organisations
6. Selling the products and/or service of one organisation to another organisation.

3.4.1 The development of your business ideas

The bow-tie diagram can also be used to develop your business idea in terms of:

- the essence of the idea
- the possible combination of ideas
- the possibility of taking a new direction with the idea.

In the following example, the idea is 'to bake cakes'; it shows all the business ideas that might emerge from this one idea.

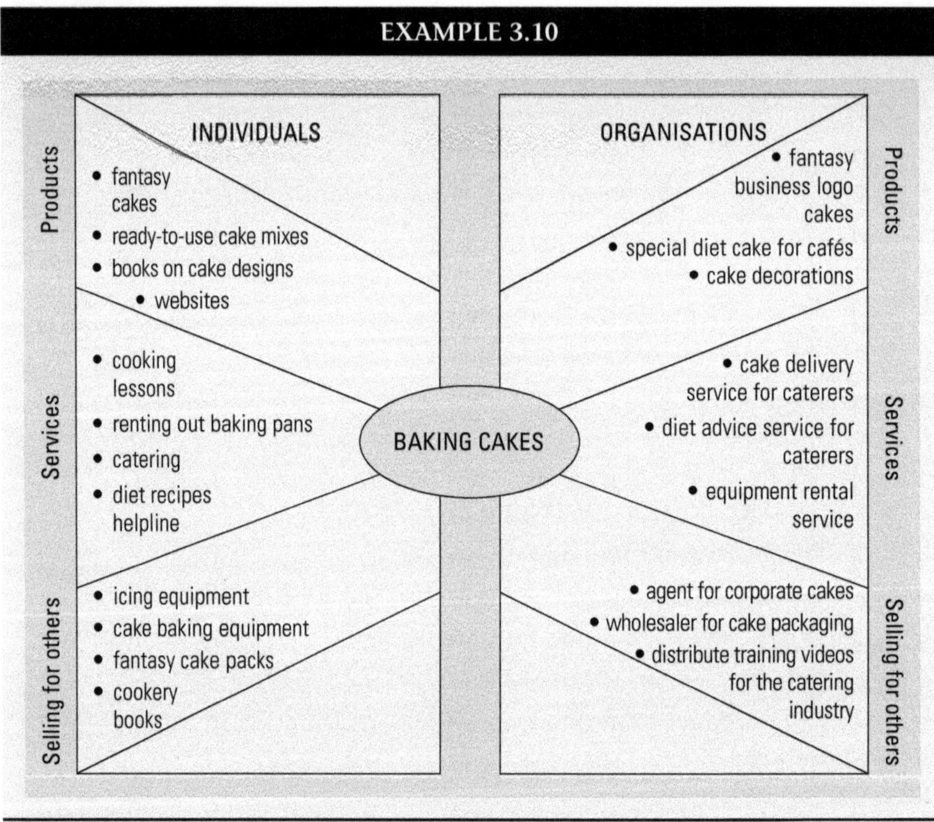

From this example, you can see that the idea 'to bake cakes' can be developed further. Here are some examples:

- baking decorative cakes (the essence of the idea)

- making cakes and making and selling cake decorations to bakeries (the combination of ideas)

- producing training DVDs for the catering industry (taking a new direction with the idea).

3.4.2 Feasibility of your business ideas

To determine whether the business idea is feasible, the entrepreneur must be able to answer the following four questions satisfactorily:

1. Do you want to do what the idea suggests?

2. Is there a market for your idea?

3. Can you meet the needs of your customers?

4. Can you advertise the idea to your customers?

To determine the feasibility of your business idea, answer the following questions by filling in a tick (✓) or a question mark (?) in the block alongside each question:

DO YOU WANT TO DO WHAT THE IDEA SUGGESTS?

- ❏ Is the idea really something that you want to pursue?
- ❏ Do you want to do business with the types of people who will be your customers?
- ❏ Do you have the health, energy and personality to pursue your idea?
- ❏ Can you cope with the long hours, few – if any – holidays, etc associated with this idea?
- ❏ Will you sacrifice the things that are important to you in order to make a successful enterprise out of this idea?
- ❏ Does your family understand the full implications of your decision to start a business?
- ❏ Do you have the support of your family and are they willing to help?
- ❏ Is this idea more important to you than any other idea that you have identified?

If you filled in any question marks (?) in the blocks above, you must ask yourself whether you really want to pursue this specific idea. In other words, do you have the motivation to achieve success with it? Think of ways to change the question marks (?) into ticks (✓) and how, for example, you can justify the ticks (✓) to your bank manager.

IS THERE A MARKET FOR YOUR IDEA?

- ❏ Do you know who your customers will be?
- ❏ Will they pay you for your product and/or service?
- ❏ Do you think there are many customers for your idea? Estimate how many.
- ❏ Will people prefer your product and/or service to those of your competitors?
- ❏ Do you think you will gain more customers in future?
- ❏ What are three advantages you have over your competitors?
- ❏ Can you prevent other people from copying your idea?

If you filled in any question marks (?) in the blocks above, you must ask yourself whether you have a market for this specific idea. Think of ways to change the question marks (?) into ticks (✓) and how, for example, you can justify the ticks (✓) to someone like your bank manager.

<table><tr><td>

CAN YOU MEET THE NEEDS OF YOUR CUSTOMERS?

❏ Do you have, or can you develop, the skills to manufacture your product and/or to provide your service?

❏ Can you provide the quantity and quality of products or give the level of service that your customers expect?

❏ Do you know how much money you can charge for your product or service?

❏ If you need someone to help you provide your product or service, do you know anyone who will be willing to do it?

❏ Do you know how much money you will need to start your business?

❏ Do you know how much money you will need to run your business in its first year?

❏ Do you personally have the money to start and run your business? How much do you still need? Where will you get the rest of the money?

</td></tr></table>

If you find any question marks (?) in the list, you must ask yourself if you can pursue this idea. Think of ways to change the question marks (?) into ticks (✔), and how, for example, you can justify the ticks (✔) to someone like your bank manager.

<table><tr><td>

CAN YOU ADVERTISE THE IDEA TO YOUR CUSTOMERS?

❏ Do you know how your customer buys this product or service?

❏ Is there a specific magazine, newspaper or journal that your customers read? What is it?

❏ Do you know of any agents or intermediaries who are currently selling to your customers? Who are they?

❏ Do you know of any businesses or organisations currently doing business with your customers? Where are they?

❏ Will these businesses or organisations be prepared to promote your idea?

❏ Can you get the names and addresses of a large number of potential customers? About how many?

❏ Do you already have various customers who have indicated that they will buy from you? How many?

</td></tr></table>

Question marks (?) in the questionnaire above are less important than the ticks (✔). If you have no ticks (✔), or only one or two, you must ask yourself if you should pursue this idea. Think of how you can turn the question marks (?) into ticks (✔), and how, for example, you can justify the ticks (✔) to someone like your bank manager.

How do you feel about your business idea now that you have answered all the above questions? Complete the rating scale in Table 3.1 by circling the number that represents your choice.

TABLE 3.1: Rating scale

LEVEL OF CONVICTION				
	VERY HIGH	HIGH	AVERAGE	LOW
Do you want to follow the idea?	4	3	2	1
Is there a market for your idea?	4	3	2	1
Can you meet your customers' needs?	4	3	2	1
Can you advertise the idea to your customers?	4	3	2	1

By adding up the numbers circled, you can reach the following conclusions from your results:

5 or less: If you are certain that it is not for you, you should restart the process of identifying ideas from the beginning.

6 to 12: If you are still undecided, you should return to your list of business ideas and consider other options.

12 and above: Your idea is feasible and must be explored further.

If you have learnt from your results above that your business idea is in fact feasible, you should investigate its viability. Since a formal viability study is expensive in terms of both time and money, it is important first to do the feasibility study as shown above. The next chapter gives a step-by-step description of investigating the viability of a business idea.

3.5   Summary

This chapter covered the first step in setting up a business, namely to identify and develop a business idea. The planning and implementation phases were also mentioned. However, these phases are discussed in more detail in subsequent chapters.

A business idea does not always have to be innovative, but it must stand out from other comparable and competitive products or services in some way. This means that the entrepreneur must be able to think and act creatively. The creative abilities of prospective entrepreneurs can be improved in various ways, such as thinking unconventionally, breaking the routine, viewing a matter from another person's perspective or using one of the various team creativity techniques.

The techniques for generating business ideas were discussed. These techniques can be divided into five broad approaches. The entrepreneur can generate a business idea from their skills, expertise and aptitudes; from common needs; from existing problems; from everyday activities; and from various other sources as well. These approaches can be adopted separately or in combination to come up with a unique idea.

A business idea should be defined in terms of its business activity and customer profile before it is evaluated and developed. This can be done through a feasibility study of the idea by matching the business ideas with questions on how the prospective entrepreneur feels about the specific idea. Business ideas must also be viable before they can be turned into a business. The viability of business ideas will be discussed in the next chapter.

SELF-EVALUATION QUESTIONS

1. Discuss the three stages of setting up a business.

2. Define the term 'creativity'.

3. Explain the characteristics or abilities that creative people have in common.

4. Distinguish between 'divergent' and 'convergent' thinking.

5. Access the internet and do an online brain dominance test. Compare the result of the test with your inclination for creativity. Such a comparison can assist you to structure your life in a way that's going to create more success and help you get where you want to be.

6. Examine the methods you can use to improve your own creativity.

7. Suppose you wish to start a new business with two friends as partners. Explain two creativity techniques to help you generate business ideas (use one of the techniques explained in this chapter and one technique that you have researched on your own).

8. Generate one business idea from your skills, one from your expertise and one from your aptitude by using the methods in this chapter.

9. Generate a business idea from a common need of people in your neighbourhood by using the method proposed in this chapter.

10. Generate a business idea from an existing problem in your area by using the method proposed in this chapter.

11. Generate a business idea from your everyday activities by using the method proposed in this chapter.

12. Name and discuss the other reference sources that can be consulted about generating ideas.

13. Generate business ideas from other sources by using the method proposed in this chapter.

14. Distinguish between a feasibility and a viability study.

15. Discuss the bow-tie diagram, its features and functions for the entrepreneur.

16. Take one of your business ideas generated in questions 6 to 10 and develop it by using the proposed bow-tie diagram.

17. Determine the feasibility of one of your business ideas by answering the following four broad questions:
    a. Do you want to do what the idea suggests?
    b. Is there a market for your idea?
    c. Can you meet the needs of your customers?
    d. Can you advertise the idea to your customers? (Justify your answers and conclusion.)

18. No commonly agreed, single definition of creativity exists. Discuss different views on creativity.

19. Discuss various uses for creativity techniques.

20. Business ideas can be discovered by accident. Debate the advantages of this statement versus the advantages of a more structured approach to finding business ideas.

21. Discuss the need for both a feasibility and a viability study in setting up a business.

REFERENCES AND FURTHER READING

Amabile, TM & Mueller, JS. 2008. Studying creativity, its processes, and its antecedents. An exploration of the componential theory of creativity. Zhou, J & Shalley, CE (eds). *Handbook of Organizational Creativity*. Lawrence Erlbaum: New York.

Barnes, A. 2017. Entrepreneurial success is impossible without creativity: 'zig when others zag' and more tips. https://dynamicbusiness.com/leadership-2/entrepreneur-profile/entrepreneurial-success-is-impossible-without-creativity-zig-when-others-zag-and-more-tips.html (Accessed 22 June 2022).

Cormack, AM & Hounsfield, GN. 1979. The Nobel Prize in Physiology or Medicine. Nobelprize.org: the Official Website of the Nobel Prize. United States. https://www.nobelprize.org/prizes/lists/all-nobel-prizes/ (Accessed 15 August 2022).

Farrell, C. 2020. Gusto: A payroll software turned 'people platform'? Assignment: Platform Business Challenges. HBS Digital Initiatives. https://digital.hbs.edu/platform-digit/submission/gusto-a-payroll-software-turned-people-platform/ (Accessed 15 August 2022).

Franken, RE. 1993. *Human Motivation*. Wadsworth: Brooks/Cole.

George, JM. 2007. Creativity in organizations. *Academy of Management Annals*, 1(1):439–477.

Mansfield, D. 2018. Brainstorming techniques: 15 creative activities to do solo or as a team. https://blog.hubspot.com/marketing/creative-exercises-better-than-brainstorming (Accessed 31 July 2018).

Markov, S. 2018. The pin card technique. https://geniusrevive.com/en/the-pin-card-technique/ (Accessed 31 July 2018).

Nieman, G & Nieuwenhuizen, C. (eds.) 2018. *Entrepreneurship: A South African Perspective,* 4th edition. Pretoria: Van Schaik.

Staff Writer. 2014. Great South African inventions. http://mybroadband.co.za/news/general/99208-great-south-african-inventions.html (Accessed 10 June 2015).

The Henry Ford. 2022. Henry Ford – Founder, Ford Motor Company. https://www.thehenryford.org/explore/stories-of-innovation/visionaries/henry-ford/ (Accessed 15 August 2022).

THE VIABILITY OF A BUSINESS IDEA

MICHAEL CANT AND ADELE VAN LILLE

LEARNING OUTCOMES

After you have studied this chapter, you should be able to:

- LO 1: Define and explain the term 'viability study'
- LO 2: Explain the term 'market research'
- LO 3: Explain the needs analysis and characteristics of customers
- LO 4: Explain the structure of the business
- LO 5: Formulate a mission statement and objectives of the business
- LO 6: Calculate the expected market share of a business
- LO 7: Calculate the income of a business
- LO 8: Calculate the expected net profit of a business
- LO 9: Calculate the break-even point of a business
- LO 10: Explain cash planning in a business

Introduction

Entrepreneurs are generally known as positive individuals. They believe explicitly in their idea or business and usually assume that the idea or business will be successful. However, it is important that the business idea be tested against certain criteria in order to enhance the chances of success. This requires proper planning. Testing or establishing the viability of the business idea is the focus of this chapter and sets out the parameters and framework of the business.

Two phases are usually linked to business planning: the first phase is to establish the viability of the business idea and the second phase is to draw up a business plan, which is depicted in Figure 4.1. Phase 1 involves assessing whether the business, as imagined, is likely to make enough money to justify its existence and to make it financially viable to proceed with the idea. A business idea is regarded or deemed viable if the entrepreneur is confident that the business can generate sufficient turnover to generate a sustainable profit. Once the idea is considered viable, a business plan (phase 2) will be drawn up. The business plan encapsulates the main elements of the viability study and is then used to secure funding for the business in order to launch the business idea.

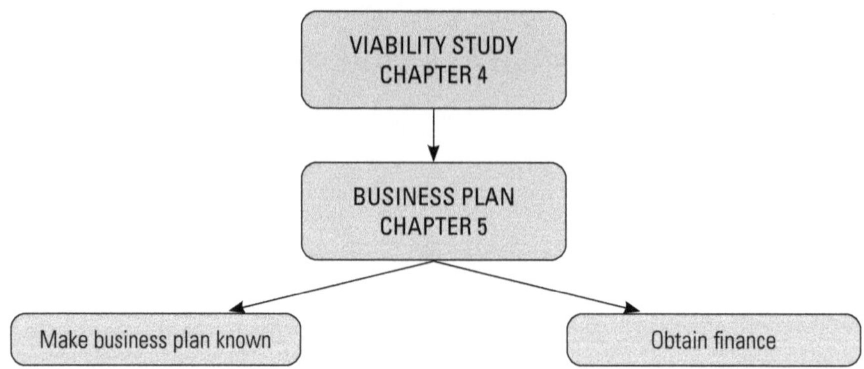

FIGURE 4.1: The planning stage in establishing a business

An idea is regarded as viable if it is deemed to be able to generate a sustainable net profit. The viability of an idea must be tested, based on certain assumptions, and on research which the entrepreneur will have had to conduct. The viability study must also make provision for unforeseen circumstances.

EXAMPLE 4.1

An entrepreneur might have an idea for a new business and after talking to friends and family believes that it is a great idea. The bank might not think so without sufficient research and feedback on the potential success of the business. How would the entrepreneur answer this? Friends and family are not the market – they tend not to be objective in giving opinions. What will the entrepreneur then do? This chapter provides a systematic approach to the viability study, commencing with market research, needs analysis and determination of the charactersitics of customers. This is followed with the determination of the structure, mission and objectives of the business. Then, the focus is turned to the financial side by calculating the expected market, income, expected net profit, break-even point and cash planning to determine the viability of a business.

LO 1: Define and explain the term 'viability study'

4.1   Viability study

Many businesses fail due to the fact that they have not made sure that the proposed or planned business is viable. The entrepreneur should ensure that the business has a good chance of survival and that it is sustainable before committing resources to it. This requires a viability study.

DEFINITION	The viability study in short is a comprehensive study aimed at establishing how profitable the business or idea is. This implies that the interest in the offerings of the business must be estimated, what the expected sales of these offerings will be at certain price levels, the expected costs associated with generating the sales, the resources available to the business, the future trends regarding the offerings and the selected target market, the strengths and weaknesses of the business, and so forth.

As is clear from the definition of a viability study, certain questions need to be answered and for this purpose information is required. The entrepreneur needs to conduct some market research in order to obtain some facts and figures to be able to estimate the size of the market, the likelihood of the market to purchase his/her product, the state of the competition, the suppliers and the costing involved, as well as the general business environment, including legal and governmental aspects applicable to the type of business. It is important that entrepreneurs are not overly optimistic at this stage and rather be on the side of caution and be a bit more conservative in their estimations.

In order for the entrepreneur to determine the market potential of the business or business idea, some steps need to be taken. The first step is to conduct market research. The second step will be to establish the needs and characteristics of the potential consumers. The mission and objectives of the enterprise should be determined as the third step, and the fourth step the entrepreneur should take is to perform a market analysis to determine the total potential market, target market and expected market share.

LO 2: Explain the term 'market research'

4.2 Market research

DEFINITION	Market research can in simple terms be defined as a structured and organised effort to collect and interpret information regarding the proposed target market and the customers on a product or service to be offered for sale in that market, and on the past, present and potential customers for the product or service. It also involves research into the characteristics, buying behaviour, location and needs of the business's target market, the industry as a whole, and the specific competitors faced.

Some of the typical questions to which the entrepreneur should find answers include the following:

- Is there a need for my product or service? (Needs analysis)
- What is the profile of the person (customer) who will buy my product or service? (Customer profile/characteristics)
- What can realistically be expected to be sold of this product or service based on the estimated market size? (Market share)
- What will the market be prepared to pay for the product or service based on the perceived value it offers and the competitive products or services already on the market? (Price analysis)
- Who would the most important competitors be and how does my offering compare to theirs? (Competitor analysis)

Based on the information gathered from the market research, some assumptions can be made. These include the following:

- the estimated sales volume that needs to be generated in order to break even (profit analysis)
- the price that the market will be prepared to pay for the product or service
- the cash-flow requirements for the business (cash flow analysis)
- the marketing approach to be followed based on a comparison with the offerings of competitors.

It is essential that the entrepreneur should do a proper needs analysis of the market and identify the characteristics of customers. The section below explains how to do this.

> **LO 3:** Explain the needs analysis and characteristics of customers

4.3 Needs analysis and characteristics of customers

Finding out and deciding on who your customers will be, what their needs and wants are and how they make their buying decisions are crucial to all businesses and need to be addressed from the start. It is imperative that there is not a disconnect between what the entrepreneur wants to offer and what the market (or the customer) really wants. The key to success is to make sure that the product or service you offer is what the customer wants and not just what you want to sell.

In order to achieve the above and hence establish if the idea is viable, information on the characteristics, needs and purchasing patterns of the potential customers is needed. Given the intense competition in the market today, reliable information is key to a successful business.

Chapter 2 explained that people buy in order to satisfy a need. However, this concept of buying to satisfy a need is not that clear or straightforward. On the one hand, a need can be very strongly felt but not easily defined, and there can be various options for satisfying that need. There is generally a distinct difference between the physical product that customers buy and the image customers have of the product. When you are about to provide a product or service to the market, you must determine which need that product or service will satisfy.

To do this, you need to be very specific about who your customers are and be able to develop a customer profile. A profile is nothing more than a description of the potential customers. You must be able to determine their distinguishing characteristics and then look for information about their location and numbers.

Having a customer profile helps businesses to make important decisions by tracking customer information, such as trends, demographics and psychological graphics. It is much easier to attract more customers when your current customers are known. With the increase in competition for customers, having a customer profile is one of the simplest ways to gain a competitive advantage.

EXAMPLE 4.2

A customer profile might include these elements:

CRITERIA	ATTRIBUTES
Gender	Male
Age	35 to 55
Education	Tertiary qualification
Annual income	R250 000 to R500 000
Attitudes	Conservative, health-conscious
Location	Gauteng

It is imperative for entrepreneurs to ensure that they understand the customers they will be serving, what their needs are and whether their offerings will be able to satisfy these needs, since customer needs form the basis of any marketing strategy. Furthermore it must be established if a sustainable profit will be made in this process. Therefore, it is important that entrepreneurs establish how they can provide the right product or service, at the right price and at the right time in order to make a profit. If not, there is no sense in entering that market.

The marketing strategy involves determining how you can provide the right products or services at the right prices; how you are going to transfer the products to the consumers (distribution); and how you are going to make the consumers aware of the products (marketing communication).

To establish the need for a product or service, you must define the market in terms of its total size, that is the group or groups of potential customers to whom you will be marketing your business. You should also identify the market where your product or service will be most widely accepted.

IMPORTANT INFORMATION

To establish the need for a particular product or service, the following typical questions should be asked when conducting market research:

1.   What are the features of the product or service?

Many entrepreneurs identify a need based on their own experiences or needs and then come upon a new idea or concept. Focusing on each aspect of a product or service and what it offers can help the entrepreneur to decide whether it meets the needs of the market. For example, think about a simple product like a shower cap. People were looking for something to keep their hair dry while showering and somebody came up with the shower cap. Today it is a product regarded as essential by many (especially females) to use when showering.

2.   Who are the major competitors? Who are the industry leaders? Who are the suppliers? Who are the other major role-players in this market?

A mistake many entrepreneurs make is to assume there is no competitor for their product – it is unique. This is a fallacy and has led to many businesses not surviving because of this assumption. Furthermore, many entrepreneurs define their competitors too narrowly. Let us look at the shower cap example above. A mistake an entrepreneur can make is to assume that the only competition will come from other shower cap suppliers. The competition can and will come from a broad spectrum of companies and products:

- **Need competition.** It must be remembered that consumers have different needs: a need for a cold drink, a takeaway sandwich, a Lotto ticket, etc. All these are competitors for the shower cap as the consumer might decide that the R100 he/she has in his/her pocket can be used to buy any of these items he/she has a need for.

- **Product competition.** As soon as the consumer decides to buy a shower cap with the R100, the other products fall away as a competitor since the consumer has made a decision to buy.

- **Brand/store competition.** At this stage the consumer needs to decide where to buy the product. Will it be at Clicks, Pick n Pay, DisChem or a Body Shop? This is where the direct competition comes in and the entrepreneur must be aware that his/her marketing strategy might just be the tactic that sways the consumer to buy from his/her store.

When one looks at the example above it is clear that consumers have different needs and that a wide range of businesses are vying for the disposable income in the pocket of the consumer. You as the entrepreneur need to give the consumer a reason to decide to buy your product.

Researching the competitive arena is very important as it forces the entrepreneur to examine the industry as a whole in order to determine its place in the market. The entrepreneur needs to identify competitors (keep in mind the example above) and how they operate and compete in the marketplace. If, for example, competition is largely in pricing, the entrepreneur may want to stay out of the market because customer loyalty is usually low in such a market. Not only must the entrepreneur look at the direct competition (other suppliers or manufacturers of shower caps) but also indirect competition. In a similar way, the entrepreneur should identify and evaluate his/her suppliers. Suppliers vary; some are reliable and deliver the right product on time and at a good price, while others do not.

3.   Which target market(s) will be most appropriate?

To identify the market segments, you as the entrepreneur need to define the market in terms of its total size and target market. Each market must be examined carefully in terms of overall size, demand and potential profitability. It is not possible to satisfy all segments: it is better to focus on the market segment that is most likely to buy your product. Determining which market segments are most attractive is called market segmentation. Market research is crucial to obtain the information needed to evaluate the target markets to focus on. In our shower cap example market research may show, for example, that females between the ages 18 and 45 are most likely to buy this cap.

After searching for answers to these questions a final list can be drawn up. This should include:

* the features of your product or service

* those customer needs that the product or service could meet

* a profile of your customers

* the competitors for the product

* the potential number of customers.

Once this information is obtained, the entrepreneur can decide on the structure of his/her business. Then he/she can also define the business and determine its objectives.

LO 4: Explain the structure of the business

4.4   The business structure

4.4.1   Types of business structures

A number of alternative structures exist for a small business. Each structure has specific characteristics and is suitable for a specific type of business. Table 4.1 lists four types of business strcutures.

TABLE 4.1: Different business structures

TYPE OF OWNERSHIP	NUMBER OF OWNERS
Sole trader or sole proprietor	1
Partnership	2–20
Company	1–50

Sole trader or sole proprietor

The sole proprietorship is the simplest and most flexible business structure. This business structure has one owner and registration of the business is not required. For example, Ricardo would like to start a computer repair shop in his town and run it from his home. When a sole proprietorship is formed, there is no distinction between the assets of the business and the owner's assets. Therefore, everything in Ricardo's house (tools, furniture and appliances) is under the same form of ownership. Ricardo will have full control and sole decision-making power over policies, profits and capital investment. In his business, there is also no distinction made between personal and business debt. If the business fails to repay a debt, the creditors have the right to seize his personal assets. For example, if Ricardo's business runs out of money to repay his bank loan, the creditor has a right to seize both personal and business assets – Ricardo's bakkie, lounge suite or his tools or all of them. The sole proprietorship is also easy to close down.

Partnership

In a partnership, the partners own the business together. A partnership can vary from two to 20 people, and is based on a written agreement prepared by the partners or by a lawyer. If a new partner joins the partnership, then a new agreement must be drawn up. The agreement needs to treat issues such as profit share and terms of termination.

As with a sole proprietorship, in a partnership there is no differentiation between the assets and debts of the owners and those of the business. Nor does the law distinguish between the assets of the different partners and debt. For example, if the business fails to repay its debts, then the creditors can legally pursue their invested funds by recovering the money from the sale of the property, whether privately or collectively owned, of the partners. This does not have to be on equal terms: the creditor may choose to focus first on the partner with the most valuable or most accessible assets. An advantage of a partnership is that it is much easier to raise finance as a partnership than as a sole proprietor.

Company

A company is formed when 1 or more people, but a maximum of 50, starting a business choose to create a separate legal entity. A company consists of shareholders and directors; shareholders refer to the owners of the business and directors refer to the managers of the business. Shareholders may act as directors, and directors may be shareholders in the company.

A company is a legal entity, therefore its debts and assets are considered to be separate from those of shareholders and directors.

4.4.2　Legal considerations

All businesses operate under a range of legal constraints and regulations. For all businesses it is important that they adhere to various legal guidelines. Amongst the most important legal guidelines are the following aspects:

- Labour practices
- Consumer protection including e-commerce protections
- Personal information protection
- Tax and municipal guidelines
- Trade rules and regulations
- Health and safety regulations
- Compliance with the Companies Act
- Financial and corruption regulations.

It is important that the entrepreneur obtain the required information and guidelines regarding these aspects in order to manage the business within the legal framework of the country and municipality.

4.4.3　Practical checklist when starting a business

The following checklist serves as a general description of the steps that a start-up company should follow:

1. Decide on the type of business entity that you wish to form: a public or private company.
2. Choose your enterprise's name and think about at least two alternative names.
3. Draw up your business plan.
4. Await your enterprise registration number from the Companies and Intellectual Property Commission (CIPC).
5. After receiving your e-number, apply for your value-added tax (VAT) number; income tax number; pay as you earn (PAYE); skills development levy (SDL); and unemployment insurance fund (UIF) numbers from the South African Revenue Service (SARS).

6. Register your logo as a trademark with the CIPC.

7. Ensure that all the enterprise's intellectual property is copyrighted.

8. If you have a unique product that you would like to patent, register this as a patent with the CIPC. Registering for copyright, patents, trademarks and designs is not compulsory for every enterprise.

The Companies and Intellectual Property Commission (CIPC) now regulates all areas related to intellectual property. The responsibilities of the CIPC include registering companies, promoting awareness of the company and intellectual property law, and monitoring compliance with financial reporting standards. Visit www.cipc.co.za for more details on the CIPC.

Once the form of business has been decided on, the entrepreneur is ready to start and manage the business. The next section focuses on the management part, commencing with the formulation of the mission and objectives of the business.

LO 5: Formulate a mission statement and objectives of the business

4.5 The mission statement and objectives of the business

In Chapter 2, the mission statement and objectives of the business were broadly described as 'what you want to achieve and how you will achieve it'. All businesses need to have a mission which gives direction to the business and specific objectives which to pursue.

Generally a business is defined according to the product or service that it wishes to sell, and by the customer profile. The definition should be neither too narrow nor too broad. If it is too narrow, it might exclude possible opportunities, but a definition that is too general can cause a lack of focus. The following questions will help you to define your business:

- Who are the customers of the business? In other words, which market/ markets will the business serve?

- Which customer needs will the business satisfy?

- How will the business satisfy these needs? In other words, which products and/or services will the business offer that will satisfy the needs of the customers?

- What technology will the business use?

4.5.1 Mission statement

By following the steps outlined in section 4.2, you have already collected the information to answer these questions. You can now proceed to define the mission statement.

A business is defined by its mission statement. A clear definition of the mission and purpose of the business makes it possible to set clear and realistic objectives. (Most companies have their mission statement on their website. See Example 4.3 for mission statements of well-known South African businesses.)

DEFINITION — A mission statement is a brief overview or description of an organisation's purpose, its market, how it serves its market through the types of products or services it provides and the technology used to serve its market. The mission statement may also include the core values, philosophies or goals of the business, which in turn can help to reflect its uniqueness and what sets it apart from the rest.

Do not underestimate the importance of a mission statement. Every entrepreneur ought to write a mission statement early on because it provides the entrepreneur and their employees with a framework and purpose.

The mission statement considers every aspect of the business: the range and nature of the products and services on offer; price, quality, service, position in the marketplace; growth potential; use of technology; and relationships with the customer, employees, suppliers, competitors and the community.

To come up with a mission statement that incorporates all the main elements of a business, answering the following questions can help in formulating a verbal picture of a business's mission:

- Why are you in business?
- Who are your customers?
- What image of your business do you want to convey?
- What is the nature of your products and services?
- What level of service do you provide?
- What roles do you and the employees play?
- What kind of relationship will you maintain with suppliers?
- How do you differ from competitors?
- How will you use technology, capital, processes, products and services to reach your goals?
- What underlying philosopies or values guided your responses to the previous questions?

EXAMPLE 4.3

Here are some mission statements of well-known South African businesses:

Woolworths: 'We are on a mission **to deliver the best in convenience, value and quality for our customers.'** (https://www.woolworthsgroup.com.au/)

Pep: 'PEP's mission is **to be the friendliest and most trusted retailer**, offering wanted products and services at the lowest prices, and our purpose is to make it possible for everyone to look and feel good. We do this through our values of honesty, passion and resourcefulness.' (https://www.pepstores.com)

BMW: BMW's mission statement is 'to be the world's leading provider of premium products and premium services for individual mobility'. (https://mission-statement.com/bmw/)

Virgin Atlantic: Virgin Atlantic mission statement is '**To grow a profitable airline, that people love to fly and where people love to work**'. (https://mission-statement.com/virgin-atlantic/)

Takealot.com: 'Takealot.com's mission is to be the most customer-centric online shopping destination in Africa. Our company is built around the simple concept that the customer comes first.' (Takealot.com, 2018)

4.5.2 Objectives

After setting the mission statement, the objectives can be formulated. The SMART framework states that the characteristics of good objectives should be that they are specific, measurable, attainable, relevant and time bound. Entrepreneurs can follow this framework to properly formulate the objectives of the business:

- **Specific:** Provide a clear description of what needs to be achieved.
- **Measurable:** Include a metric with a target that indicates success.
- **Attainable:** Realistic, yet it should still provide a challenge.
- **Relevant:** Should relate to the business's mission and strategic goals.
- **Time bound:** Should have a specific time limit.

DEFINITION   An objective is what the business wants to achieve within a set period of time.

EXAMPLE 4.4

This is an example of an objective that a restaurant might have:

Not a SMART objective: Decrease food costs by 20%.

A SMART objective: To meet restaurant's food cost reduction goal of 20%, management supervision will focus on food waste reduction, including spoiled food and scrap, by 10% per month for six months, then 6% for six months, monitored every two weeks.

The second stated objective is a SMART objective because: The objective is specific, as the focus is on waste as a cost reduction method; measurable as results will be monitored regularly; realistic with improvement targets that decrease over time; relevant to a higher-level goal; and time bound to a total of one year.

Objectives are necessary for measuring progress. They are usually adjusted over time, based on changes that take place in the industry and the environment.

Defining your mission statement and objectives clarifies the nature and purpose of your business. The process of defining also helps you calculate your market share so that you can assess whether your product or service can be marketed profitably.

Your predictions should be realistic. Whatever you do, do not be too optimistic; it does not help to mislead yourself. If you are too optimistic, it could lead to failure.

LO 6: Calculate the expected market share of a business

4.6　Market analysis

4.6.1　Calculating the total potential market

To do a market analysis, the entrepreneur needs to determine the total potential market, the target market, the size and positioning of the market as well as the expected market share.

It is not easy to describe and evaluate a potential market. Most entrepreneurs, working with unquantified information, have no alternative but to assume. However, when you identified the need for your product, you collected much of the information needed to segment your market.

Begin by dividing the potential market into segments:

EXAMPLE 4.5

A restaurant in Johannesburg cannot cater for all the needs and tastes in the food market. The entrepreneur must, therefore, select a specific segment of the total market to service. For instance, the entrepreneur must decide on what food to sell – Italian or Mexican food. This choice is then called the target market and consists of customers with similar needs and tastes.

Establishing your target market involves three steps:

1. Market segmentation
2. Evaluation and the target-market decision
3. Market positioning.

Step 1: Market segmentation

DEFINITION	Market segmentation is the division of the total potential heterogeneous consumer market into smaller homogeneous groups that have similarities or characteristics in common.

Market segmentation involves identifying and dividing an overall market into subgroups or segments with similar needs. The market can be subdivided into the following segments:

- **Demographic segmentation:** Demographic features such as age, gender, race, religion, family size, income and education are useful for describing customers with similar needs.

EXAMPLE 4.6

My target market will be men in the 25 to 35 age group, of Indian descent and in the higher income group.

- **Geographical segmentation:** Segmenting geographically means segmenting based on location. It is not always possible to serve all potential customers and therefore you may decide, for example, to focus initially only on Cape Town and Hermanus.

- **Psychographic segmentation:** Customers can be grouped on the basis of their personality traits, values, attitudes, interests and lifestyle – for instance, those who enjoy the outdoors and like 4 × 4 driving.

- **Behaviouristic segmentation:** This is based on actual consumer buying behaviour. Some behaviours include readiness to purchase, level of loyalty, frequency of interactions with your brand, occasions and benefits sought. Some people may prefer seafood to Italian food, some prefer quiet, romantic settings, while others prefer lively music and dancing while they dine. Some only eat out on special occasions and others do so at least once a week. Customer behaviour varies.

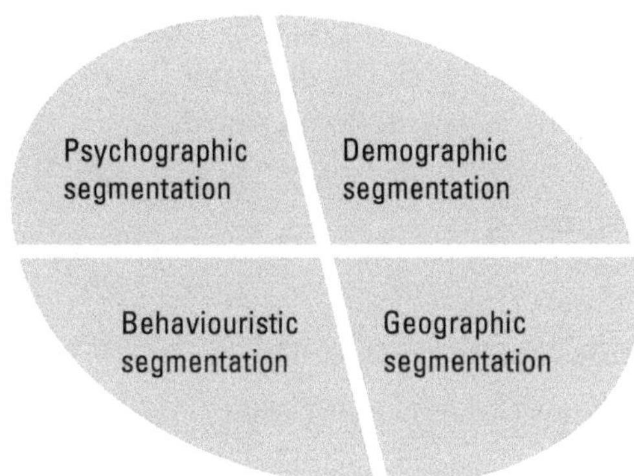

FIGURE 4.2: Market segmentation

IMPORTANT INFORMATION

Because there are various ways to segment the market, you must select the appropriate criteria for your product or service. See Table 4.2 for some examples.

TABLE 4.2: Criteria for segmentation

PRODUCT OR SERVICE	CHARACTERISTICS	SEGMENTATION
Safety doors	Cares for the family, needs protection while on holiday	Psychographic
Sports goods	Used for exercise and entertainment	Demographic and psychographic
Restaurants	Visited for celebrations and entertainment	Behaviouristic

Step 2: Evaluation and the target-market decision

Having grouped the total market into segments, you must select one segment as your target market and focus your marketing campaigns on it. The choice should be governed by such things as the following:

- **Accessibility:** Will you be able to reach your consumers? (For advertising purposes)

- **Measurability:** Can you determine the number of consumers in the segment? (Size and to generate enough profit)

- **Profitability:** Can the consumer pay the price for your product that will enable you to make a profit?

If most customers in an area prefer Indian to Chinese food, for example, and there is not an Indian restaurant in the area, it is logical to provide Indian food as this will generate more sales and greater profits.

Step 3: Market positioning

If you choose more than one segment as your target market, design a different marketing campaign for each segment. For example, if one market segment prefers Indian food and the other one Chinese food, the advertising to each of these segments will differ. In summary, it is usually impossible for an entrepreneur to focus on the entire market. It is preferable and realistic to focus on a single segment only. We call this 'the target-market decision'. Successful entrepreneurs go for a large share in one segment, rather than a small share in the total market.

4.6.2   Calculating the size of the market

Here is the traditional method for estimating the market size of your target market:

Number of customer units	(a)
Average annual gross income per unit	(b)
Total income for area	(a) × (b) = (c)
Percentage (%) of income spent on item	(d)
Potential rand value for item	(c) × (d) = (e)
Realistic percentage (%) of entrepreneur's market share	(f)
Rand value of entrepreneur's market share	(e) × (f) = (g)

EXAMPLE 4.7

John intends selling snacks and soft drinks on a part-time basis at a university where there are 880 students and the average annual income per student is R1 000. On average, the students spend 20% of their income on snacks and soft drinks. John is convinced that he will attract 5% of the market share. There is a cafeteria on campus and other competitors off campus. What is the potential rand value of this market?

Answer

1.	Number of customers	880
2.	Average annual gross income	R1 000
3.	Total income of students for the area	(880 × R1 000) = R880 000
4.	Percentage spent on items	20%
5.	Potential rand value of market	(R880 000 × 20%) = R176 000

6. Realistic percentage of market share   5%

7. Rand value of John's market share   (R176 000 × 5%) = R8 800

If John is happy with his rand value, he can continue with his business plans. If he is unhappy with the market share, he should research another business idea.

IMPORTANT INFORMATION

To retain market share or even increase it, the entrepreneur should market products in such a way that attracts customers from other competitors.

EXAMPLE 4.8

How do we determine the number of units, the average income and the percentage spent on items? This information is available in newspaper reports, information provided by the government and municipalities, and data from the private sector and academic research bureaus.

4.6.3   Determining the target market

DEFINITION   A target market is a specific group of consumers at which a business aims its products and services.

The target market refers to a specific market segment or segments (discussed in the section above) at which the entrepreneur will direct the products or services. To determine the target market, the entrepreneur will first have to find out what part of the total potential market is served by the competitors. Make a list of competitors and determine which segment in the market is their target market. Once this is done, deduct their market share from the total potential market.

A thorough analysis of the competitors is necessary. Determine, for example, who they are, where they are, what products they sell and what prices they charge. The entrepreneur now needs to determine how well he or she will be able to compete with them. This can be done by means of compiling a SWOT analysis(see Figure 4.3).

DEFINITION   A SWOT analysis is a framework used to evaluate a business's competitive position and to develop strategic planning. A SWOT analysis assesses a business's internal strengths and weaknesses, as well as its external opportunities and threats.

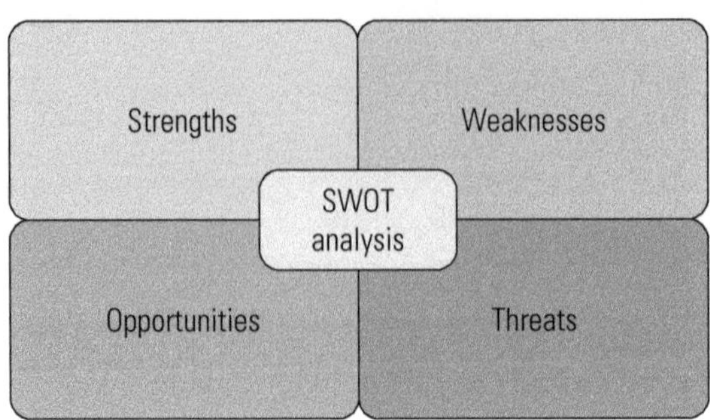

FIGURE 4.3: SWOT analysis

4.6.4 Calculating the expected market share

SWOT analysis is a list the entrepreneur must compile of the business's strengths, weaknesses, opportunities and threats (see Figure 4.3). As per the definition, strengths and weaknesses are internal to your business, therefore come from the micro environment, and the opportunities and threats are external, therefore come from the market and macro environments.

Strengths are what a business excels at and what differentiates it from competitors, for example a strong brand, loyal customer base, a strong balance sheet and unique technology. Weaknesses prevent a business from performing at its best. These are areas where the business needs to improve to remain competitive. For example, a weak brand, high turnover, high levels of debt, an inadequate supply chain, or lack of capital. Opportunities are favourable external factors that can provide a competitive advantage. For example, if a country cuts tariffs, a car manufacturer can export its cars into a new market, increasing sales and market share. Threats are external factors with the potential to harm a business. For example, a drought is a threat to a wheat-producing business, as it may destroy or reduce the crop yield. Other common threats include rising costs for materials, increasing competition and tight labour supply.

The next step in the planning process is to determine the expected market share for your product or service (see Figure 4.4). Market share needs to be calculated as accurately as possible because it will be used as a basis for estimating potential income. The potential market should not be overestimated, as this will give a a false sense of expected income.

To calculate the expected market share, estimate:
- the product's or service's total potential market
- competitors' portion of the market
- the market portion you can expect to sell to (known as your target market).

There may be times when a business cannot satisfy the demand for a product or service because its capacity restricts the production volumes (the numbers of items that can be produced). At other times, the economy may decline, so the pressure on funds and credit will restrict customers and thus demand. Because the economy and external environment change, you should determine your expected market share in varying circumstances.

DEFINITION   Market share is the percentage of a market (either in number of units sold or revenue) accounted for by each business.

The expected market share is that part of the target market that a business will be able to serve based on its production capacity and the state of the economy.

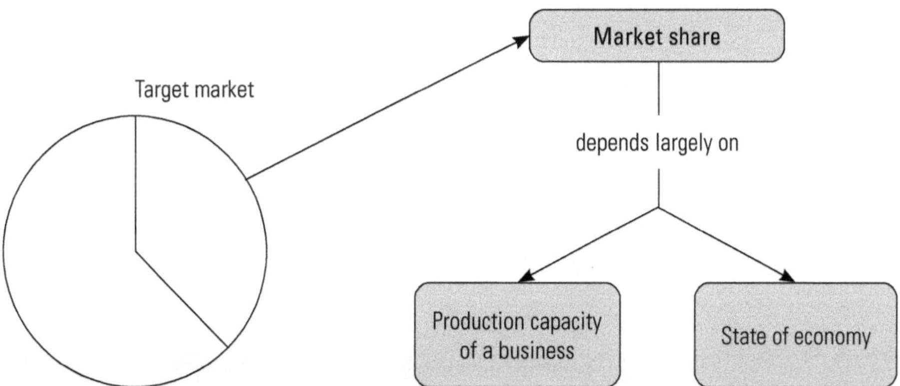

FIGURE 4.4: Estimating the expected market share

Calculating market share based on total revenue has four steps:

1. Select a fiscal period.
2. Calculate the business's sales.
3. Calculate industry sales.
4. Divide business sales by industry sales and multiply by 100.

The following example illustrates the calculation of market share. Wonder Automotive is a domestic business that manufactures non-luxury vehicles. The business earned R14 million of revenue in 2020. The domestic automotive industry as a whole had R400 million of revenue. Dividing R14 million by R400 million, you get a market share of 0,035 or 3,5%.

Calculating market share based on units sold has four steps:

1. Select a fiscal period.
2. Calculate the total number of units sold by the business.

3. Calculate the total number of units sold by the industry as a whole.

4. Divide the total number of units sold by the business by the total number of units sold by the industry and multiply by 100.

The following example illustrates this calculation. In 2020 Wonder Automotive sold 560 vehicles. The domestic auto industry as a whole sold 8 000 vehicles. Dividing 560 by 8 000, you calculated that Wonder Automotive had a market share for units sold of 0,07 or 7%.

It is not easy to estimate the expected market share, but it is essential to do so as accurately as possible to calculate a realistic potential income. To be realistic and reduce your risk you should calculate in terms of three scenarios:

- a prosperous one

- a conservative one

- the most likely one.

The average of the three scenarios will be the one to work from. Remember that if you manipulate or inflate the figures, you will only be fooling yourself! You should then calculate the profit in each scenario and judge whether it is worth going ahead with the business idea (see Figure 4.5). (See section 4.8 for an explanation of how to calculate your profit.) This kind of calculation is imperative if you wish to secure financing from a source such as a bank.

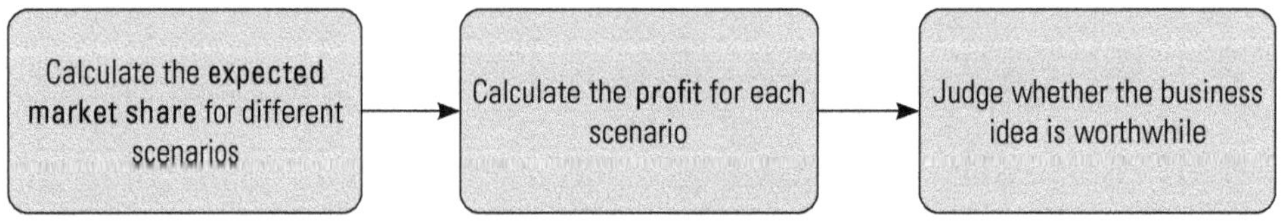

FIGURE 4.5: Calculating whether the business idea is worthwhile

The second part of the viability study is to determine the profit potential of the business idea, which involves the following two steps:

1. calculating the expected income

2. projecting the net profit of the business.

LO 7: Calculate the income of a business

4.7   Calculating income

To calculate the potential income for your business, you should work out the selling price of your product or service. To do this, establish precisely what costs will be incurred in manufacturing and selling the product. You must first know the total cost per unit (cost price) before you can calculate the selling price (see section 4.7.1).

The selling price should at least cover all the costs; otherwise, the business will show a loss from the start and will not survive.

After the cost per unit has been established, the next step in calculating the selling price is to add a percentage profit (mark-up) to the cost price. The total cost price + profit = selling price.

If you add a mark-up of 40% and the product's cost price is R10, the product will sell at R14 (see Example 4.9).

To calculate the selling price by adding a mark-up to the cost price, you must add the percentage mark-up to 100 and then divide it by 100. You then multiply the answer by the cost price of the product.

EXAMPLE 4.9

If you have a 40% mark-up and the cost price of the product is R10, the selling price will be:

40 + 100	=	140
140 ÷ 100	=	1,40
1,40 × 10	=	R14,00 (selling price)

Put differently, the selling price would be R10 plus R4 = R14,00

If you have a 60% mark-up and the cost price of the product is R20, the selling price will be:

60 + 100	=	160
160 ÷ 100	=	1,6
1,6 × 20	=	R32,00 (selling price)

In deciding what the mark-up and selling price should be, you should know the market price, that is, what your competitors are charging for the same product. If your market analysis has shown that the market is price sensitive, you must charge a competitive price. If the market is not price sensitive, then you may get away with charging a higher price if the product can be differentiated.

4.7.1 Calculating the cost price of the product

When calculating the cost price it is crucial to classify the costs as:

* variable and fixed costs
* direct and indirect costs.

Variable and fixed costs

Variable costs are fixed per unit but vary in total. This means that the costs rise with the number of units manufactured (see Figure 4.6). For example, if the raw materials in a product cost R1 and ten products are manufactured, the total variable cost is R10. If 20 products are manufactured, the total variable cost is R20, but it is still R1 per product.

Variable costs can be shown on a graph as follows:

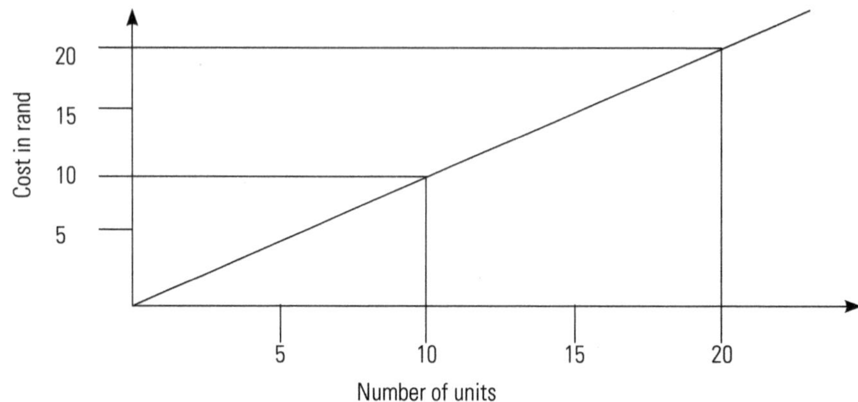

FIGURE 4.6: Variable costs

Fixed costs are fixed in total but vary per unit (see Figure 4.7). The rent for a factory is R100 (point A) – a fixed cost. This means that if you make ten units of your product, each one costs R10 to make. If 20 products are manufactured, the total fixed cost is still R100 (point B), but each unit costs R5 to make.

Fixed costs can be shown on a graph as follows:

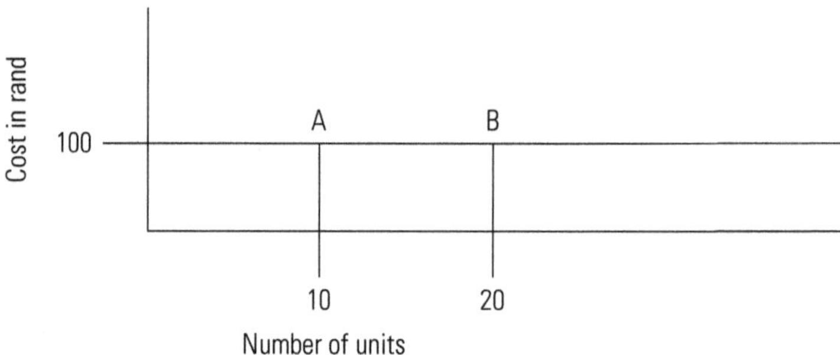

FIGURE 4.7: Fixed costs

By adding up the fixed and variable costs, one can calculate the product's cost price, as shown in Figure 4.8.

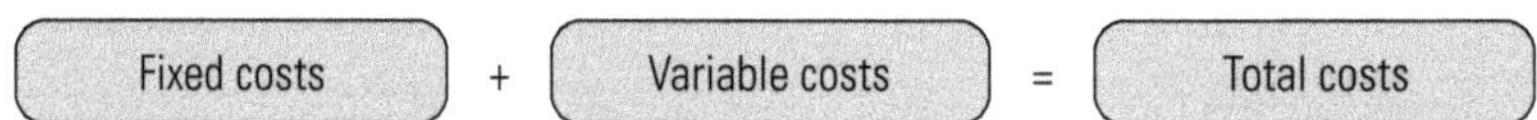

FIGURE 4.8: Calculating total costs

Direct and indirect costs

Direct cost is a price that can be directly tied to the production of the product or service. Examples are the raw materials used to manufacture a product and wages of labourers who are directly involved in manufacturing the product.

Indirect costs (also called overheads) cannot be allocated directly to a product. Examples of these are the rent of the factory, electricity, water, depreciation and indirect wages (like the salary of the owner).

Calculating the total costs per unit of the product

There are various ways of calculating the cost of a product in a business, depending on the type of business. There are specific differences in calculating the cost per unit for the following types of businesses:

* manufacturing business

* commercial business

* service business.

Calculating the total costs per unit of a product for a manufacturing business
The total costs of a product in a manufacturing business are manufacturing costs plus commercial overhead costs.

* **Manufacturing costs:** These consist of direct labour costs (the wages), direct material costs (the costs of raw materials) and manufacturing overhead costs (indirect costs) (see Figure 4.9).

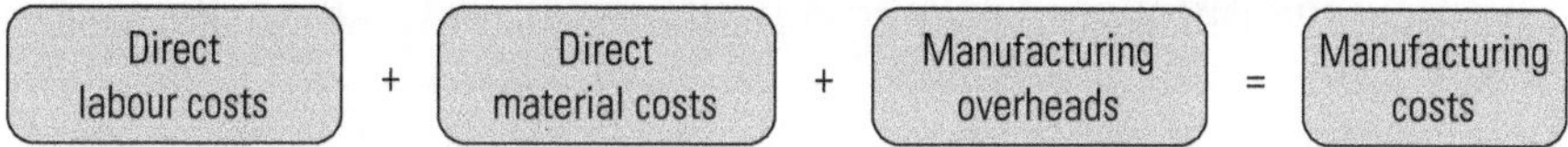

FIGURE 4.9: Calculating manufacturing costs

* **Commercial overhead costs:** These consist of administrative and marketing overheads (see Figure 4.10). The administrative overheads are all costs related to the administration of the business functions, such as human resources, finance and management. Marketing costs are all the costs incurred in marketing the product, such as advertising.

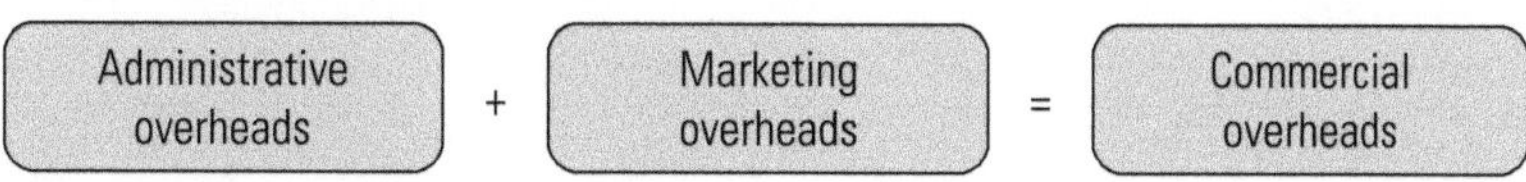

FIGURE 4.10: Calculating commercial overheads

Follow these steps to calculate the total costs of one unit of a product (see Figure 4.11):

- Calculate the direct costs of the materials used to manufacture one unit of a product.
- Calculate the direct labour costs needed to manufacture one product unit.
- Calculate the indirect costs per product unit: add manufacturing, marketing and administration.
- Divide this total by the number of products manufactured during the period that the costs were incurred.
- Add the costs together to get the total costs per unit.

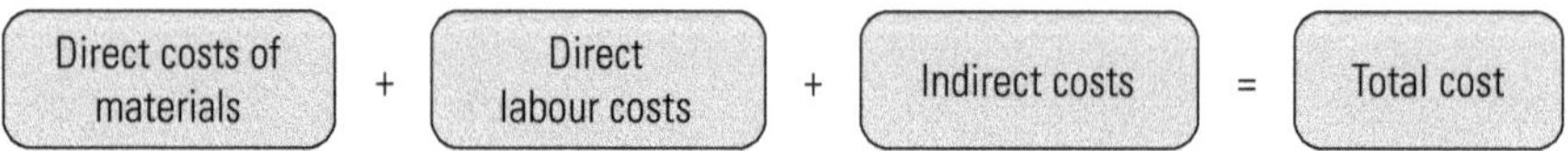

FIGURE 4.11: Costs per unit for a manufacturing business

Calculating the total costs per hour for a service business

The products for sale are intangible in a service business: knowledge and skill. An example of this is the repair of equipment. In this kind of business, an hourly rate for labour must be calculated.

Follow these steps to calculate the total costs of one unit of product (see Figure 4.12):

- **Calculate the number of business hours per month:** This is the number of hours the business operates. For example, daily from 8:00 to 17:00 (in other words, 9 hours per day):
  6 days per week × 9 hours per day = 54 hours per week × 52 weeks = 2 808 hours per year ÷ 12 months = 234 hours per month
- **Calculate the cost per hour:** To do this, calculate the total expenses for a month, for example rent on the building, salaries and rental on office equipment. Suppose it is R10 000 a month. Divide the total costs by the number of working hours per month: R10 000 ÷ 234 hours = R42,73 per hour. This means that you cannot charge less than R42,73 per hour for your services.

FIGURE 4.12: Total costs of a product for a service business

Calculating the total costs per product for a commercial business
A commercial business does not manufacture products but buys finished products then resells them at a higher price. The total costs for a product in a commercial business are made up of the purchasing costs of the product to be sold (the cost of sales) plus the commercial overhead costs (see Figure 4.13).

Cost of sales per unit + Overheads per unit = Total costs per unit

FIGURE 4.13: Total costs of a product for a commercial business

4.7.2 Calculating the selling price

The price you can charge for your product or service is directly influenced by the competitors' prices for the same kind of product or service. If your products or services are much more expensive than those of your competitors, you will lose customers. Your products or services can only be more costly than those of competitors if you offer more benefits: this means that the market must perceive that they are getting more value for money and that you are the one who offers it.

To determine what you can charge for your product, make a list of your products and then establish what your competitors charge for similar ones. List the competitors' strengths and weaknesses alongside those of your business and compare the two lists, as done in Table 4.3.

TABLE 4.3: Comparison of strengths and weaknesses

YOUR OWN BUSINESS	COMPETITOR'S BUSINESS
List of products and prices	List of products and prices
1.................... R....................	1.................... R....................
2.................... R....................	2.................... R....................
3.................... R....................	3.................... R....................

In this way, you establish what the highest and lowest prices are and what price range (the prices charged for the product or service in general) applies to the product or service. If a business has exceptional strengths, this can justify higher prices. The opposite is also true: if the business has many weaknesses, it will be obliged to charge lower prices than its competitors.

This comparison helps you decide what you can charge for your product or service. Remember that you may never charge less than the total cost of a product or service unless that product is used as a 'loss leader' to attract customers to the store.

Once the selling price has been established, the potential income and the net profit from the product sale can be calculated.

The final part of the viability study of the business idea is based on the following financial projections: to calculate the expected net profit (Pro Forma Statement of Comprehensive Income (previously this was called the Pro Forma Income Statement) and the break-even point; and to do cash planning by preparing a cash budget (cash forecast)).

LO 8: Calculate the expected net profit of a business

4.8   Calculating the expected net profit

After establishing the costs and mark-up for your product, you are now ready to test the viability of the business. To be viable, the business idea must be profitable. To establish turnover, you must multiply anticipated unit sales by the anticipated selling price and then deduct likely costs. The difference will be your profit. If the income exceeds the expenses, you will be making a profit. If not, you will be making a loss. Net profit is calculated by drawing up a 'Pro Forma Statement of Comprehensive Income'.

DEFINITION	A Statement of Comprehensive Income (previously known as the Income Statement) is a summary of the income and expenditure of a business over a specific period of time.

The main entries on a Statement of 'Financial Performance' with 'Comprehensive Income' are as follows: Sales (units sold multiplied by the selling price) – cost of sales = gross profit/income – expenses = net profit/income.

DEFINITION	A Pro Forma Statement of 'Financial Performance' with 'Comprehensive Income' is drawn up using estimated figures.

The purpose of drawing up a Pro Forma Statement of 'Financial Performance' with 'Comprehensive Income' is to calculate the net profit for the three scenarios discussed in determining the expected market share, namely for a prosperous one, a conservative one and for the most likely one.

EXAMPLE 4.10

An example of a Statement of Comprehensive Income (previously known as the Income Statement) is provided below.

Perfect Solution Co

Statement of 'Comprehensive Income' for the year ended 28 February 2022

		R	
Revenue		970 000	
Less: Cost of sales		701 000	
Inventory:	1 March 2021	90 000	
Add:	Purchases	700 000	
	Freight on purchases	6 000	
Inventory:	28 February 2022	796 000	

	R
Gross profit (970 000 – 701 000)	269 000
Add: Discount received	4 000
Total	273 000
Less: Selling, administrative and general expenses	178 450
Freight on sales	4 000
Discount allowed	3 000
Commission to sales personnel	9 000
Salaries and wages	95 450
Stationery and postage	3 000
Bad debts	2 500
Insurance	6 000
Sundry expenses	16 000
Auditor's remuneration	6 500
Director's remuneration	15 000
Loss on sale of equipment	2 000

Depreciation	16 000
Profit from operations (273 000 – 178 450)	94 550
Investment income	5 000
Listed investments	2 000
Unlisted investments	3 000
Less: Finance costs	(14 300)
Interest on bank overdraft	(2 000)
Interest on mortgage loan	(4 800)
Interest on debentures	(7 500)
Profit before tax	83 450
Income tax (29%)	24 200,50
Net profit for the year	59 249,50

LO 9: Calculate the break-even point of a business

4.9   Calculating the break-even point

For any business, the gross sales volume level needed to reach the break-even point must be calculated.

DEFINITION   Break-even is the point at which total revenue and total costs are equal, alternatively, the number of units that must be sold for the income and expenditure to be equal.

The break-even analysis is a technique for analysing how revenue, expenses and profit fluctuate with changes in sales volume.

In other words, this is the point where all costs and expenditures are covered. At this point, the net profit will be equal to R0, which means neither a profit nor a loss is shown.

Begin the break-even analysis by establishing all your business's fixed (overhead) expenses. Since most are monthly, do not forget to include quarterly or annually paid expenses, such as payroll taxes or insurance. For example, if your annual insurance charge is R9 000, use a twelfth of that (R750) as part of your monthly budget. With the semi-variable expenses, such as phone charges, travel and marketing, use a figure you expect to spend every month.

EXAMPLE 4.11

For the purpose of a model break-even calculation, let us assume that the fixed expenses for Perfect Solution Co are as follows:

Administrative salaries	R1 500
Rent	R800
Utilities	R300
Insurance	R150
Taxes	R210
Telephone	R240
Car expense	R400
Supplies	R100
Sales and marketing	R300
Interest	R100
Miscellaneous	R400
Total	R4 500

These are the expenses that your gross profit must cover. Assuming that the gross profit margin is 30%, what sales volume must you achieve to cover these expenses? The answer, in this case, is R15 000; 30% of that amount is R4 500, which is your target figure.

The two critical numbers in these calculations are the total fixed expenses and gross profit margin percentage. If your fixed expenses are R10 000 and your gross profit margin is 25%, your break-even figure must be R40 000.

Therefore, the break-even point can be calculated in rand value and units. The break-even point in units' formula is calculated by dividing the total fixed costs of production by the price per unit less the variable costs to produce the product. And the formula for the break-even point in rand value can be calculated by dividing the total fixed costs by the gross profit margin percentage multiplied by 100.

Along the way, expenses tend to creep into direct and indirect categories. Therefore, it is important to look at your profit and loss statement every six months or so and recalculate your break-even target figure.

4.9.1 Ways to lower the break-even volume

There are four main ways to lower your break-even volume; two of them involve cost control (which should always be your goal!):

1. **Lower direct costs to increase the gross margin:** Be more diligent about purchasing material, controlling inventory, or increasing your labour

productivity by more cost-effective scheduling or adding more efficient technology.

2. **Decrease the amount of your fixed expenses:** Be careful to cut expenses with an overall plan in mind. You can cut too deeply or too little and cause distress among workers, or you may pull back marketing efforts at the wrong time: that may give out the wrong signal to the market and customers.

3. **Increase selling prices without significantly decreasing the number of units sold:** Most entrepreneurs are reluctant to do this because they think business will fall off. More often than not, this does not happen unless your market is highly price-sensitive, and then you have probably already become volume-driven.

4. **Improve the sales mix:** Sales mix is the relative proportion of a business's sold products. The sales mix is essential because a business's products and services usually have different degrees of profitability. For example, a custom furniture business intends to sell 100 furniture units in the current year. The planned sales mix is 20 furniture units of low profit, 50 furniture units of medium profit, and 30 furniture units of high profit. Therefore, the planned sales mix is 20%, 50%, 30%.

The custom furniture business intends to have a small operating loss with this volume and sales mix. However, the total number of units sold was only 95 units. Having five fewer units sold could mean a substantial operating loss. However, the business's loss (or profit) depends on the actual sales mix. Suppose the actual sales indicate that 15% of 95 units sold were the low-profit units, 45% were the medium-profit units, and 40% were the high-profit units. Thus a more favourable sales mix (15-45-40 instead of 20-50-30) could result in an operating profit even with five fewer units sold.

If you are in the typical niche-type small business, you can raise your prices by 4–5% without your customers noticing. The effect on your profitability can be startling.

EXAMPLE 4.12		
Look at the difference in the following example:		
Volume	R15 000	
Direct cost	R10 500	(70%)
Gross profit	R4 500	
Raising the price by 5% would result in this change:		

Volume	R15 750	
Direct cost	R10 500	(67%)
Gross profit	R5 250	

You will have increased your margin by 3% and in so doing lowered the total volume you need in order to break even.

4.9.2 The aim is profit

You are in business to make a profit, not just break even. However, knowing your break-even point allows you to manage your business more effectively:

- You can allocate the sales and marketing efforts to get you to the point you need to reach. For example, you know that you want to sell five extra cars by the end of this month, so you can advertise more than usual.

- You can control costs if you predict a month where demand typically declines. Such months occur in most companies, for example in the retail industry straight after Christmas. However, losses can be minimised if you plan accordingly. Remember that a few bad months can quickly wipe out accumulated profits.

- You can maximise profits by knowing and understanding the elements of your break-even figure.

LO 10: Explain cash planning in a business

4.10 Cash planning: the cash budget (cash forecast)

Up to this point, we have stressed the importance of sustaining profits over time.

IMPORTANT INFORMATION

Do not attempt any business venture if you cannot sustain profits over time.

Making a profit is not enough. While you should be able to sustain profits over a period, it is important to have enough cash available to manage the business on a day-to-day basis. You may be making a net profit but lack sufficient ready funds to meet expenses as they arise. Then you cannot continue trading but will go bankrupt and have to close your business. You will be in a state known as 'technical bankruptcy'. Therefore, to continue in business, you must have an adequate cash flow to meet your expenses as they arise.

To overcome this problem, you must pay close attention to planning the actual flow of money in and out of your business. The priority is to know how much actual money you will receive and on what dates. The same applies to expenses: how much and when will you have to spend. A tool you can use to help with this cash planning is the cash budget.

DEFINITION The cash budget is a formal plan for estimating the cash flow of a business (future receipts and payments of cash) over a specific period of time, which could be weekly, monthly, quarterly or annually.

EXAMPLE 4.13

You would not buy new furniture for your home without enough cash or at least a solid plan to cover a personal loan from your bank. Your business needs the same careful handling of expenses. No matter what type or size, all businesses need to develop a plan for their expected cash intake and spending. This is the cash budget.

4.10.1 The purpose of cash budgeting

The cash budget allows you to establish how much cash flows into and out of your business. The cash budget is used to assess whether the business has sufficient cash to continue operating over the given time frame. However, its primary purpose is to provide the status of the business's cash position at any point in time. The budget can also:

- be used to plan for short-term credit needs
- be presented to your bank or other financial institution to demonstrate your proper financial planning
- help you predict months when your business might have a cash shortfall
- highlight problem areas in your payment schedule – for example, payments to creditors may be lumped together on one date. More careful planning could spread this evenly throughout the entire year.

4.10.2 Consistent budgets

Cash budgeting is a continuous process that can be checked for consistency and accuracy by comparing budgeted amounts with amounts that can be expected and by using typical ratios or financial statement relationships.

For example, your assessment will estimate the payments you have made to your suppliers of merchandise or materials; those to employees for wages and salaries; and other payments that you are obliged to make. These payments can be scheduled by date to take advantage of any available discounts and avoid overlooking any payments as they become due. Cash collections from customers and other expected cash receipts can also be estimated and scheduled by date.

With careful cash planning, you should be able to maintain an adequate cash balance without holding excessive balances of non-productive cash.

EXAMPLE 4.14	
A cash budget	
The following is an example of a cash budget for the ABC Company.	
Cash budget for 90 days	
Beginning cash balance	R1 320 000
Add:	
Estimated collections on accounts receivable	R1 750 000
Estimated cash balances	R1 250 000
	R1 320 000
Deduct:	
Estimated payments on accounts payable	R1 800 000
Estimated cash expenses	R1 150 000
Contractual payments on long-term debt	R1 150 000
Quarterly dividend	R1 250 000
	R1 150 000
Estimated ending cash balance	R1 170 000

4.10.3 Analysing the cash budget

An analysis of the financial statements of the ABC Company shows the following:

- Accounts receivable remain at about R500 000 throughout the year. Therefore, there is no seasonal fluctuation in sales.

- Accounts receivable turns over six times a year, or once every 60 days.

- The inventory throughout the year remains at about R800 000 and turns over every 90 days.

- Accounts payable remains at about R400 000 and turns over eight times a year: about once every 45 days.

- There is an accounts receivable collection period of 60 days and an average balance outstanding of R500 000. It appears that R750 000 is the amount that should be collected on the receivables in 90 days.

- Cash sales should amount to about R250 000 if the inventory of R800 000 valued at cost turns over once in 90 days and if the average mark-up is about R200 000. Therefore, if an inventory of R1 000 000 at retail turns over once every 90 days and R750 000 flows through accounts receivable, approximately R250 000 must be sold on a cash basis.

- Cash payments for expenses are estimated to be R150 000 in the next 90 days. This figure can be roughly checked by referring to the Statement of Financial Performance's (Income Statement's) expenses. A rough measure of the cash expenses can usually be obtained by using the operating expenses less any non-cash expenses such as depreciation. For example, if there is no seasonal factor, the total amount divided by four should be an approximate check on the amount budgeted for the next 90 days.

4.11 Summary

This chapter dealt with the first phase of the planning stage of the business, which is to establish the viability of the business idea. Phase one involved assessing whether the business would have market and profit potential to make it financially viable to proceed with the idea.

Performing a viability study is an integral part of the planning process for any business. The reason for carrying out such a study was discussed, and the various steps in the process were explained.

The viability study's market potential determinants involve: doing market research to establish exactly who your customers will be; whether your product or service will satisfy their needs; who your competitors will be; how to set up a mission and objectives for your business; and how to do a market analysis. The above discussions achieved Learning Objectives 1–5.

The viability study's profit potential determinants included the necessity to calculate your income: to do this, you need to calculate the cost price and selling prices of your product or service, and from those figures establish what your profit will be. You must draw up a cash budget and calculate the break-even point of the business. The above discussions achieved Learning Objectives 6–10.

The reason for the viability study has been stressed. Remember, to be viable, your business idea must be profitable and sustainable over a specific period.

SELF-EVALUATION QUESTIONS

1. Discuss what a viability study is and why it is important.

2. How will you establish whether you have the product or service the customer wants?

3. What kind of information forms part of a customer profile?

4. Define a market for a product of your choice.

5. Name and discuss the questions that need to be asked to see whether there is a need for a particular product or service.

6. What is the purpose of a mission statement?

7. What questions need to be answered in formulating the mission statement?

8. Name the characteristics of objectives.

9. What is the purpose of a SWOT analysis?

10. Why is it important to calculate the expected market share?

11. What do you need to calculate the expected market share?

12. How can you establish a target market?

13. Define indirect costs.

14. Describe what constitutes manufacturing costs.

15. What is the formula to determine the cost per unit for a manufacturing enterprise?

16. What is the formula to determine the total costs of a service for a service enterprise?

17. What is the formula to determine the total costs of a product for a commercial enterprise?

18. How is net profit calculated?

19. Define the break-even point for a business.

20. What are the four ways to lower the break-even point for a business?

REFERENCES AND FURTHER READING

Averkamp, H. 2022. What is the sales mix? https://www.accountingcoach.com/blog/what-is-sales-mix (Accessed 23 February 2022).

Cant, MC. (ed). 2011. *Marketing: An Introduction*. Cape Town: Juta.

Cant, MC, Brink, A & Machado, R. 2005. *Pricing Management*. Claremont: New Africa Books.

Cant, MC, Van Heerden, CH & Ngambi, HC. 2010. *Marketing Management: A South African Perspective*. Cape Town: Juta.

CIPRO. Companies and Intellectual Property Registration Office. 2011. Cipro's beginner's guide to our services. http://www.cipro.gov.za/products_services/beginners_guide.asp (Accessed 28 March 2011).

Entrepreneur. 2018. Market research. https://www.entrepreneur.com/encyclopedia/market-research (Accessed 1 August 2018).

Entrepreneur. 2018. Target market. https://www.entrepreneur.com/encyclopedia/target-market (Accessed 1 August 2018).

Entrepreneur. 2022. Break-even analysis. https://www.entrepreneur.com/encyclopedia/break-even-analysis (Accessed 23 February 2022).

Entrepreneur Media, Inc. 2015. 10 questions to answer when writing your mission statement. https://www.entrepreneur.com/article/241954 (Accessed 1 August 2018).

Entrepreneur Media, Inc. 2018. Mission statement. https://www.entrepreneur.com/encyclopedia/mission-statement (Accessed 1 August 2018).

Erasmus, B, Rudansky-Kloppers, S & Strydom, J. 2016. *Introduction to Business Management*, 10th edition. Cape Town: Oxford University Press.

Fin24. 2011. Body to replace Cipro launched. http://www.fin24.com/Economy/Body-to-replace-Cipro-launched-20110418 (Accessed 31 July 2018).

Hull, P. 2013. Answer 4 questions to get a great mission statement. https://www.forbes.com/sites/patrickhull/2013/01/10/answer-4-questions-to-get-a-great-mission-statement/#5155ad7667f5 (Accessed 1 August 2018).

Indeed. 2021. How to calculate market share (with examples). https://www.indeed.com/career-advice/career-development/how-to-calculate-market-share. (Accessed 23 February 2022).

Kenton, W. 2021. Strength, Weakness, Opportunity, and Threat (SWOT) Analysis. https://www.investopedia.com/terms/s/swot.asp (Accessed 23 February 2022).

Mundy, K & Bullen, SG. nd. Estimating market potential: Is there a market? https://plantsforhumanhealth.ncsu.edu/extension/marketready/pdfs-ppt/business_development_files/PDF/estimating_market_potential.pdf (Accessed 23 February 2022).

Nieuwenhuizen, C. 2001. *Basics of Entrepreneurship*. Cape Town: Juta.

Strydom, JW. (ed). 2004. *Introduction to Marketing*. Cape Town: Juta.

Takealot.com. 2018. More about our journey. https://www.takealot.com/about/our-journey (Accessed 1 August 2018).

Tardif, L. 2018. Examples of SMART goals and objectives. https://business.lovetoknow.com/wiki/Examples_of_SMART_Goals_and_Objectives (Accessed 1 August 2018).

Tuovila, A. 2021. Cash budget. https://www.investopedia.com/terms/c/cashbudget.asp (Accessed 23 February 2022).

Legislation

Companies Act 71 of 2008

THE BUSINESS PLAN

ALEX ANTONITES

LEARNING OUTCOMES

After you have studied this chapter, you should be able to:

- LO 1: Understand the purpose and principles of a business plan
- LO 2: Identify and describe the users of a business plan
- LO 3: Explain the business model
- LO 4: Explain the business plan
- LO 5: Discuss the technological assistance in drafting a business plan
- LO 6: Explain the structure of the business plan
- LO 7: Indicate guidelines for writing a business plan
- LO 8: Write a business plan

Introduction

The current economic climate in South Africa and in many emerging economies worldwide causes increased levels of business failure. The Covid-19 pandemic contributed even more to an alarming level of business distress and consequent failure for many. The Russia–Ukraine conflict commencing early 2022 further contributed to uncertainty in the business environment and further possible failures for many businesses due to rising oil and fuel prices globally. South Africa's unemployment rate also reached a new critical level of 35% in 2022 that signals even more individuals having to start their own businesses. Entrepreneurs need to devise a way either to start a new business or to develop a new business managerial plan that mitigates risk and is geared to growth (as compared to potential failure). In Chapter 4 we discussed the first half of business planning, namely how to do the viability study. If you have decided that your business idea is indeed viable, then you can move on to the next step: the business plan. This plan is a critical element in every phase of the entrepreneurial route to success involving risk management and growth.

The business plan plays a pivotal role in the entrepreneurial process. If you, as an entrepreneur, apply for start-up capital or a government grant or if you tender for a government contract, one of the first questions you will be asked is if you have a business plan. Also, private equity providers, like venture capitalists, require a comprehensive plan with the core purpose to indicate how their investment will return high yields. Another method in micro and small business financing is crowdfunding, and even this requires a well-structured business plan. This suggests that a business plan is the only platform for judging your business, albeit on paper. Remember that the business opportunity is the core focus of entrepreneurial venturing. A business plan is a picture and blueprint of how the entrepreneur will participate in the entrepreneurial process. It shows any reader (even yourself) that you have created clear architecture for the building to follow.

Let us assess two entrepreneurial cases:

Case study 1

Fab Letsholo, a young and dynamic entrepreneur from the North West province, involved herself in designing technology applications for the informal sector. She studied informatics but also did some online courses to develop applications for both iOS and Android. Having grown up in a family whose members were teachers or in mining, she had no business background, exposure or insight.

One evening while watching TV, she saw an amazing programme about the informal sector and how some spaza shops actually make a lot of money, albeit without any formal infrastructure. As a child, she had bought bread at a spaza on her way back home from primary school, thus the environment was familiar. She suddenly realised that her IT skills might actually make a difference.

Fab started developing an application that will assist spazas with their accounting. She spent hours working on an operational prototype. After six months a final product was ready for roll-out.

Case study 2

Peter opened a small outlet near his home to sell basic consumer goods like maize, milk and cold drinks, and also provided a public phone. As sales increased, he realised that an opportunity existed for making yoghurt from unsold milk, and a nearby farmer offered all his surplus milk. He decided to expand and opened a small yoghurt factory. Peter was then also able to expand his sales to the large number of spaza shops in his region. Because the business was doing well, Peter was able to expand again and build a cheese-making unit.

All these decisions were based on well-researched opportunities in the marketplace and on sound financial planning. Because of this planning, and given the vigorous growth of the business, Peter is now investigating the possibility of buying the dairy farm that currently supplies him.

The above are typical scenarios drawn from the lives of potential and emerging entrepreneurs. The first case is in that critical phase where a business plan will map a route to success. All the elements exist: setting up the business, marketing the application, establishing the business, defining the financial requirements and making projections. The second example shows existing entrepreneurial performance and success. A cornerstone of success is in-depth planning: the business plan is an integral part of this planning process.

5.1 The purpose and principles of the business plan

The primary objective of the business plan is to develop a blueprint to define your business.

The plan is:

- a meticulous route map to entrepreneurial success
- a document that clarifies the product or service you want to sell or render
- a detailed written document stipulating how you will address all the business activities to exploit the identified business opportunity
- an indication of how the new business's strategy will be operationalised
- a planning document that explores and indicates the route to follow into the future
- a document that you, the entrepreneur, should formulate by yourself.

5.1.1 A blueprint for the business

The business plan serves exactly the same purpose as an architect's plan, which includes a detailed building schedule with quantities and costs of all the items necessary to complete the work, such as bricks, mortar, wood, steel and labour. In the same way, the business plan lists all the facets of the proposed business.

5.1.2 A flexible document

The business plan is not a static or fixed document; it is a dynamic planning instrument that should be updated regularly to take account of changes in the business environment. For instance, customer buying patterns may shift towards healthier eating (eg a trend towards eating organic food); new competitors may enter the market with new, comparable products (eg organic food with recyclable packaging). Your suppliers may also change their approach (eg no more credit offerings, which could have a negative impact on cash flow). Timely adaptation to these changes is the only way for your business to survive.

5.1.3 A plan developed by the entrepreneur

The only way to understand your business properly is to develop your own business plan. This is the best way to end up with a unique plan that suits you and your business, and offers you the opportunity to think strategically and operationally of all the elements of your business. While it is possible to use the services of an external consultant, this may not be as effective and you may end up with an 'off-the-shelf', generic product.

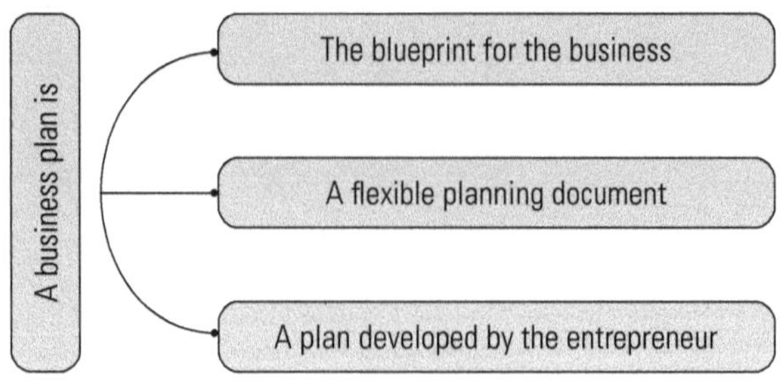

FIGURE 5.1: The business plan

LO 2: Identify and describe the users of a business plan

5.2   The users of the business plan

A secondary objective of the business plan is to acquire finance from a financier (eg a commercial bank or financial agency). It can also serve as a marketing document to present to potential investors or venture capitalists. The larger suppliers of raw materials may similarly ask to see the plan to evaluate your reputation, substance and financial position.

Some entrepreneurs use the business plan to motivate their employees. By communicating the long-term planning and goals, they hope to give their staff a greater sense of 'ownership' and involvement. The risk is making your plans too widely known: if staff resign, their possession of commercial intelligence is an asset your competitors might want to secure. A business plan is a confidential document: therefore whoever reads it should sign a non disclosure agreement to preserve confidentiality.

Figure 5.2 summarises the other users of a business plan.

FIGURE 5.2: Potential users of the business plan

LO 3: Explain the business model

5.3   The business model

5.3.1   Value creation

A key component of any sound business plan is the design and formulation of an effective business model. All the elements of the business model are eventually translated into the business plan. Why is a business model so important? A business model is a clear description of how you and your business will, in the first place, create value for customers (in the modern world with its unique market dynamics, people want more value than before) and, second, what contributes to the effectiveness of the business venture in creating value for customers. The following elements should be included in your business model (and it is advisable to formulate these before you commence with the business plan):

The value proposition

This section indicates clearly what you sell or render of value to the customer. The unique selling proposition (USP) is also included, meaning how you will differentiate your offering from competitors. It is also critical to ask and address the following questions:

- What are we selling (product description)?
- In selling this product, what problem do we solve for customers?
- What value do we create with the offering?

Target customers

Many entrepreneurs think that their products will be used by 'everyone'. This is a popular mistake. Entrepreneurs should focus on a specific group of customers with more or less the same needs to be satisfied. This is the target market.

Channels

How do you get the product to the target customer? At first you must make the selected target market (or markets) aware of your existence. Your advertising or communication strategy should be formulated here. After that, the distribution channels (eg if it is in retail, the customer will walk into your store, so the chain is short; but if you have a business-to-business proposition, a logistical process should be designed). Over the past decade, the introduction of social media as a high-impact channel to the market changed the way entrepreneurs do business. The Covid-19 pandemic led to a huge increase in online shopping, which further contributed to the impact of social media as a high-impact channel. Various social media offerings currently exist that could assist any entrepreneur in taking their product to the marketplace. It not only enables you to focus on the exact market segments, but also offers a medium that is highly cost effective. The following platforms are highly efficient for small business entrepreneurs.

GRAPH 5.1: Top social network platforms 2022 (most popular social networks worldwide as of January 2022, ranked by number of monthly active users)

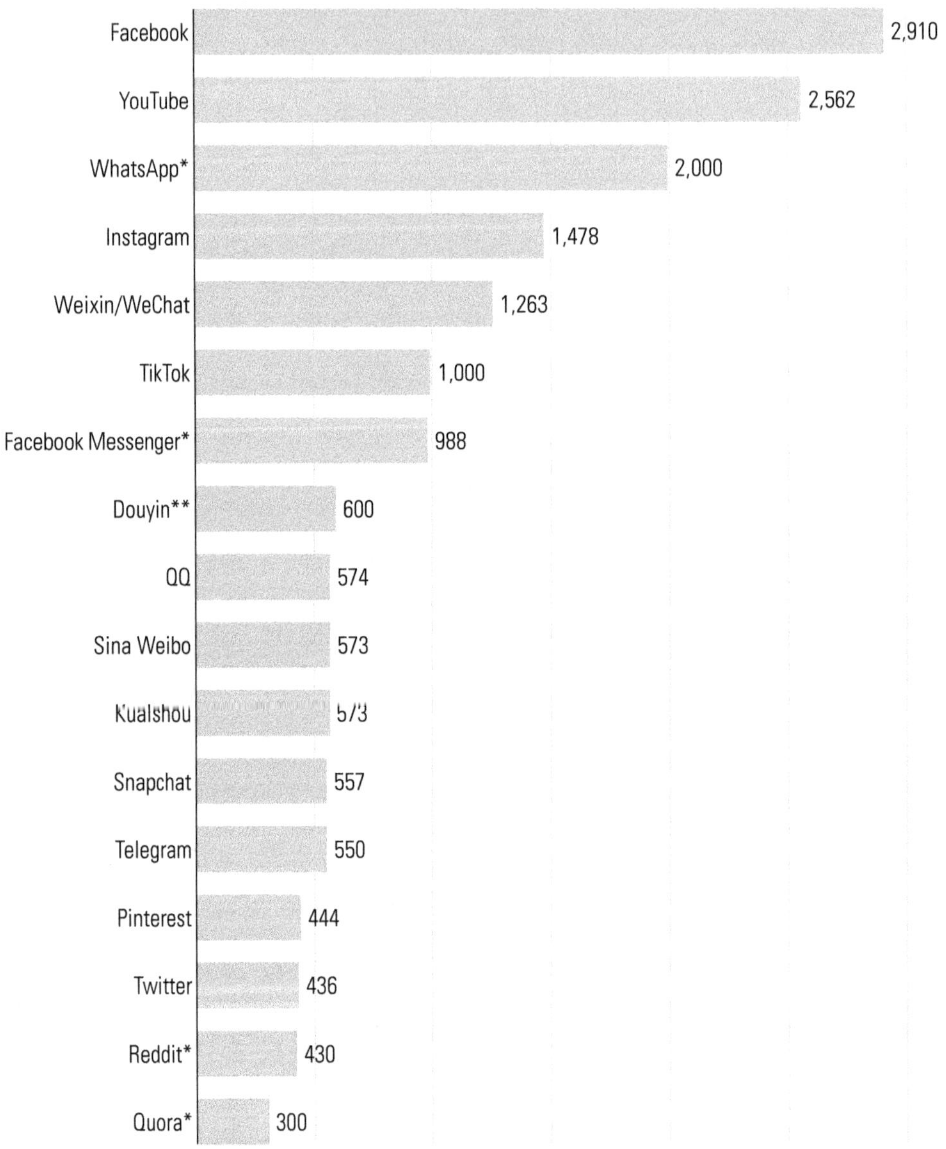

Source: https://www.statista.com/statistics/272014/global-social-networks-ranked-by-number-of-users/

It is also critical to indicate in your business model why you have chosen the specific platform/s in terms of the exact value it/they add to your channel.

Customer service

How do you:

- attract new customers
- create loyalty
- get them to tell others (word-of-mouth referral)?

Exceptional customer service is not negotiable for a small business. It offers you the opportunity to differentiate your business, not only with competition but also with bigger businesses. Customer service of this nature should unconditionally include friendly service, in-depth product knowledge and rapid feedback to customer requests (eg service/product quotes or technical queries).

Income model

How will your business make money? A brief description of your income streams (eg selling goods, rental or an annuity model). Remember that this section feeds directly into your *financial plan* as the final part of the final business plan (including the cost structure section of your model). It therefore guides your thinking and design of a suitable financial plan.

External stakeholders

In this section you analyse all the external entities that might contribute to the efficiency of your business. The starting point is your suppliers of input goods (eg raw material or packaging material); government agencies (eg Small Enterprise Development Agency (Seda) or Small Enterprise Finance Agency (Sefa)); and organisations (eg your chamber of commerce).

Operational activities

The operational process in your business should be described well as it will contribute to effective cost analysis and management. Here you need to describe all the primary activities (eg customer orders, deposit payments, design and manufacturing, packaging, distribution and delivery) as well as all the support activities (eg human resource management and IT support).

Key resources

Any business is driven by factors of production or input resources and their supply. Although the degree of influence depends on the nature of your business, the following core resources are normally present in a generic small business venture:

- employees (human capital, like sales people)
- finance capital (eg starting and working capital)
- raw materials

- intellectual property (eg a patent)
- technology (tools and equipment).

Cost structure

The cost structure of any small business is critical in many ways. Knowing what it is will not only help determine the viability of the start-up, but also support the process of determining the pricing of products for customers. The two fundamental cost types are fixed costs, meaning they are features of the business, like salaries and rental, and variable costs, which change in relation to production volumes.

Your business model then prepares you for completing the entire business plan.

> **LO 4:** Explain the business plan

5.4   The business plan

The business plan, compiled after the model, is a planning instrument that describes the entrepreneurial process and how the entrepreneur will implement it. However, the plan is not the nucleus of success: it is a map, not the road. Many potential entrepreneurs may think that if a business plan is on paper, success should follow. But business success and entrepreneurial performance depend on more than this. Initially, you would have identified a feasible opportunity in the market environment. As discussed, and explained in Chapter 4, you would then have undertaken a viability study. A viable opportunity therefore precedes the written business plan. The viability study creates a platform for writing the business plan.

IMPORTANT INFORMATION

Remember that undertaking a viability study precedes the business plan and contains valuable information to assist in drafting the plan.

In Table 5.1, the opportunity is distinguished from the business plan.

TABLE 5.1: From the opportunity to the business plan

Identify and evaluate the opportunity	• Creation and length of opportunity
	• Real and perceived value of opportunity
	• Risk and returns of opportunity
	• Opportunity versus personal skills and goals
	• Competitive situation

Develop the business plan	<ul><li>Title page</li><li>Table of contents</li><li>Executive summary</li><li>Description of business</li><li>Description of industry</li><li>Marketing plan</li><li>Financial plan</li><li>Production/operations plan</li><li>Organisation plan</li><li>Summary</li></ul>
Determine the resources required	<ul><li>Existing resources available</li><li>Resource gaps and available supplies</li><li>Access to needed resources</li></ul>
Manage the small business	<ul><li>Management style</li><li>Key variables for success</li><li>Identification of problems and potential problems</li><li>Implementation of control systems</li></ul>

Figure 5.3 graphically demonstrates how the various components of a business plan contribute to business success

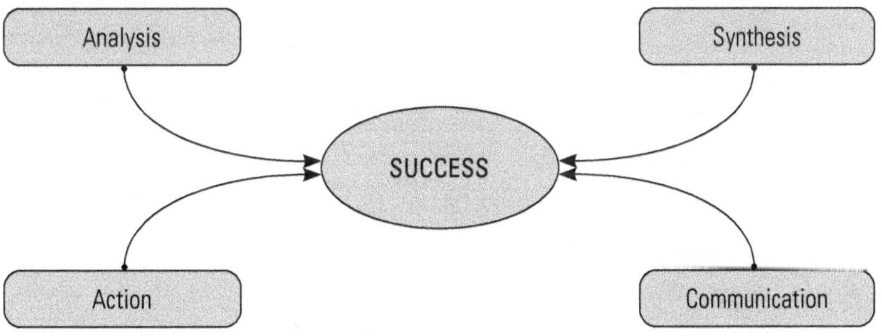

FIGURE 5.3: The mechanisms of a business plan that support business success
Source: Adapted from Wickham (2001:197)

All the components of the business plan contribute to the eventual success of the business in the future. Figure 5.3 illustrates certain key mechanisms that underwrite business success:

- **Analysis:** In-depth research should be conducted prior to the compilation of a plan. The entrepreneur should, to name a few, gain insight into customer preferences (eg pricing information), the capital requirements for starting up (eg to lease property) and trends in the market (eg rapid changes in technology). The internet became a massive support resource in analysing almost all the components of the market and macro environments.

- **Synthesis:** The relevant information obtained from the analysis/research process feeds into the final business decision-making, conveyed in the business plan (eg opening an online retail store instead of opening up a physical store in a big mall with extremely high rental costs).

- **Communication:** A business plan communicates the blueprint of the business to selected stakeholders (eg financiers, investors or customers) and should therefore represent a professional document transferring the required message and information to the reader.

- **Action:** The eventual success of the business is highly dependent on the accurate implementation of the business plan. This is by far the most difficult part of the entrepreneurial process and asks for a detailed plan that will ease the decision-making process in the hard reality of practice.

LO 5: Discuss the available technological assistance in drafting a business plan

5.5 Technological assistance in drafting the business plan

In modern times, more and more forms of support and enhancements evolve from the internet and contribute to the efficiency of all entrepreneurs. This also applies to the compilation and refinement phases of the business plan. The following sites will also help you build a well-structured business plan, drawing on examples, templates and applications:

- https://www.gov.za/faq/finance-business/where-do-i-get-assistance-establish-small-business
- https://www.businessplanpro.co.za/
- http://www.sabusinessplans.co.za/
- http://www.bplans.co.za/business-plans/
- https://www.absa.co.za/business/starting-my-business/setting-up-my-business/drafting-a-business-plan/
- https://www.smetoolkit.businesspartners.co.za/en/content/business-plan
- https://www.entrepreneur.com/article/334261
- https://www.oldmutual.co.za/articles/business-plan-template
- https://www.liveplan.com/business-plan-bank-loan
- https://www.guidantfinancial.com/blog/how-to-write-a-business-plan-for-a-loan/

(As the entrepreneur, you should always remember that these software and support tools still require your intellectual input.)

LO 6: Explain the structure of the business plan

5.6 The structure of the business plan

The structure of a business plan is important but should always follow your strategy (formulated in the business model). It is advisable to structure your plan so that it meets the needs of your industry and the needs of the potential reader or user. A service-rendering business, for instance, is less likely to have a production plan. Adapt the structure and style to the needs of the reader and remember that you will be the first reader and user. The following three basic structures (see tables 5.2, 5.3 and 5.4) are widely used. Also have a look at the Appendix for a relevant sample of a South African's entrepreneur's business plan.

TABLE 5.2: Structure 1: The comprehensive structure for a business plan

1. COVER PAGE	
• Name and address of business	• Name of entrepreneur
• Nature of business	• Statement of finance needed (optional)
• Statement of confidentiality of report	
2. EXECUTIVE SUMMARY	
3. INDUSTRY ANALYSIS	
• Current and potential trends	• Competitive analysis
• Market segmentation	
4. BUSINESS DESCRIPTION	
• Background of entrepreneur or team of entrepreneurs	• Core products or services
• Unique selling point/s	
5. PRODUCTION PLAN	
• Operational process	• Physical outlay of manufacturing facility

• Machinery and equipment	• List of suppliers and their core competencies
6. MARKETING PLAN	
• Pricing	• Distribution
• Promotion	• Sales forecasts
7. ORGANISATIONAL PLAN	
• Legal form of ownership	• Description of shareholders or members
• Management structure and role description	• Background of managers or project leaders (if applicable, eg managers will be appointed)
8. ASSESSMENT OF RISKS	
• Assessment of internal weaknesses	• Market risks
• Business risks	
9. FINANCIAL PLAN	
• Projected statement of comprehensive income	• Projected statement of financial position
• Projected cash-flow statements	• Break-even analysis
• Sources of finance and the application thereof	
10. ADDENDUM	
• Marketing research information	• List of suppliers and their core competencies
• Letters related to the business	• Contracts and patents/copyright (if applicable)
• Primary goals of the business	• Uniqueness of the product/service

TABLE 5.3: Structure 2: The general structure for a business plan

1. COVER PAGE	
• Potential problems	• Obstacles and risks
2. EXECUTIVE SUMMARY	
• Potential problems	• Obstacles and risks

3. BUSINESS DESCRIPTION

• General description of business	• Industry background
• Primary goals of the business	• Uniqueness of the product/service
• List of suppliers and their core competencies	

4. MARKETING PLAN

• Marketing research and analysis	• Target market
• Market size	• Competition
• Potential market share	• Marketing strategy
• Pricing	• Advertising and promotions

5. LOCATION

• Advantages	• Zoning
• Taxes	• Proximity to suppliers
• Transportation issues	

6. MANAGEMENT

• Management team – key personnel	• Legal structure: shareholding or membership agreements; employment agreements; ownership
• Board of directors, advisers, consultants	

7. FINANCIAL PLAN

• Financial forecasting	• Profit and loss
• Cash flow	• Break-even analysis
• Cost controls	• Budgets

8. CRITICAL RISKS

• Potential problems	• Obstacles and risks
• Alternative courses of action	

9. MILESTONE SCHEDULE	
• Timing and objectives	• Deadlines

TABLE 5.4: Structure 3: An alternative structure for a business plan

1. COVER PAGE
2. EXECUTIVE SUMMARY
3. BACKGROUND AND PURPOSE OF BUSINESS
4. MARKETING
5. COMPETITION
6. DEVELOPMENT, PRODUCTION AND LOCATION
7. MANAGEMENT
8. FINANCIALS
9. RISK FACTORS
10. HARVEST OR EXIT

| 11. SCHEDULING AND MILESTONES |
| 12. APPENDICES |

It must be stressed that the structure of your business plan should be geared to the class of reader. Structure 1 is an all-inclusive plan and suitable to be used as the blueprint of the business.

For financing institutions, your plan, structure and emphases will have to be structured to meet their requirements and concerns.

LO 7: Indicate guidelines for writing a business plan

5.7 Guidelines for writing a business plan

The structure and the content of your business plan will reflect on your business. The following guidelines may assist with writing the actual plan:

- Keep the plan respectably short. Stick to a concise but clear plan (not exceeding 30 pages).

- Organise and package the plan to engage and guide the reader. Follow a logical structure with a professional presentation (for instance, a cover page with the company name, logo and contact details, presented in such a way that the reader is interested in what follows).

- Gear the plan to the future, clearly indicating what you intend to do, and support this with a trend analysis and forecasting.

- Avoid exaggeration. Do not inflate the potential of the business, but be realistic about sales and revenue estimates.

- Highlight critical risks. This shows the reader that you are aware of potential problems, and it gives you the opportunity to explain how you will manage them.

- Describe an effective entrepreneurial team. The management description is of critical importance: it should convey the skills and contribution of each member of your team in terms of overall objectives of the business.

- Do not over-diversify. The plan should focus only on that segment of the market you identified during your market research (see Chapter 4).

- Identify the target market. Give particulars of your target market and explain how you performed your market research.

- Keep the plan written in the third person. Rather use 'he', 'she', 'they' or 'them' than 'I', 'we' or 'us'.

- Capture the reader's interest. Financial institutions receive many requests for funds. Concentrate on clearly defining the uniqueness of your proposed business.

LO 8: Write a business plan

5.8   Writing a business plan

You are now ready to start writing your business plan. As an example, we are going to use Peter's business referred to earlier in this chapter. The full plan forms the Appendix at the end of this book, but a summary of the information that should appear in your plan follows:

5.8.1   Cover page

The cover page should contain the proposed name of the business, its address and relevant contact details. It should also be dated with a date relevant to the content and existence of the plan.

5.8.2   Confidentiality agreement

A business plan contains confidential information on the business make-up, core competencies, competitive advantages and financial condition of the business venture and the entrepreneur. It is, therefore, critical to safeguard the content by asking the readers to sign a confidentiality agreement.

5.8.3   Table of contents

The table of contents guides the reader to and through the information, and should be accurately linked to the content of the plan (insert all the main and subheadings accompanied by the relevant page numbers).

5.8.4   Executive summary

This summarises the plan in two to three pages. It provides an overview of the status of the business; the basic description of what the business is and of its owners; potential and current customers; and a brief summary of the finances of the business. It also indicates the purpose of the business plan – for example, financial requirements or investment potential in terms of shareholding. It is advisable to complete the executive summary only after the entire business plan has been finalised.

5.8.5 Business description

This section details what the business intends to do in the market; the industry in which it will operate; industry characteristics and trends; and what the business sells or intends to sell to its customers (the unique characteristics of the product or products). It furthermore points out short-, medium- and long-term objectives.

5.8.6 Marketing plan

The marketing plan illustrates how the product or products will reach customers. This section describes the intended target market; what type of media will be used to attract its customers; and what pricing strategy will be applied. It also explains the proposed distribution strategy and competition. The best way to compile a marketing plan is to base it on proper marketing research findings.

5.8.7 Location

This section of the plan explains the specific decisions that were made in establishing the business. These would include: proximity to suppliers and customers; the zoning of the property; and transport factors. Another relevant factor is the availability of skilled labour as a resource to the business. The information in this section should be based on the findings of a feasibility study.

5.8.8 Management

This section must show how management will achieve its business objectives. It should illustrate the human competence and experience in the business; details of the management team and organisational structure (if applicable); the legal structure; and available professional support.

5.8.9 Financial plan

To a certain extent, the financial plan is the central component of the business plan. It specifies resources required and how these will be financed and managed. For an established entity, historical financial performance information should be described, or the pro forma or projected financial forecasting in terms of the future expectations.

The nature and purpose of the business plan will state a time frame for forecasting (for instance, three or five years ahead). The main body of the financial plan should contain the projected cash flow and statement of comprehensive income as well as the statement of financial position. A break-even analysis must also support the plan. (The cash-flow statement examples of Peter's business project a one-year period, only because of space constraints in this book.) It is advisable, however, to provide realistic projections over a much longer period – three years.

5.8.10 Critical risks

The risk assessment section must explain all potential risks to the normal, future operations of the business. These risk factors may exist in variables in the macro environment (such as legislation), the market environment (such as competition) and the micro environment (such as managerial issues). The reader must understand how the management team will manage all potential threats. It explores all the 'what if' issues.

5.8.11 Appendices

Appendices should include all the additional detailed documentation mentioned in the body of the plan, such as:

- market research
- curricula vitae
- product specifications and photographs.

5.9   Summary

Every entrepreneur should remember the saying that, 'If one fails to plan, one plans to fail.' A business plan is primarily a planning instrument and a blueprint of the business venture, whether new or old. The structure of the plan should be adjusted to the nature of the business and its purpose (for instance, attracting finance). Always keep the reader in mind with specific reference to their level of knowledge. The length of the plan is less important than the quality of the content. All the components of the plan should communicate with one another and be strengthened by a well-structured executive summary. Remember, this business tool is flexible and needs continuous adaptation and improvement to accurately describe a changing business!

SELF-EVALUATION QUESTIONS
1. Explain the reasons for drawing up a business plan.
2. List three users of the business plan.
3. What is the executive summary in the business plan?
4. List critical risks associated with your own business idea.
5. Draft a business plan for your own business idea.

REFERENCES AND FURTHER READING

Nieman, G & Nieuwenhuizen, C. 2019. *Entrepreneurship: A South African Perspective*, 4th edition. Pretoria: Van Schaik.

Osterwalder, A, Pigneur, Y & Smith, A. 2010. *Business Model Generation: A Handbook for Visionaries, Game Changers, and Challengers.* Hoboken, NJ: Wiley.

Spinelli, S & Adams RJ. 2015. *New Venture Creation: Entrepreneurship for the 21st Century.* Boston: McGraw-Hill.

Wickham, PA. 2001. *Strategic Entrepreneurship: A Decision-Making Approach to New Venture Creation and Management*, 3rd edition. Harlow, England: Financial Times Prentice Hall.

6

SETTING UP A BUSINESS

CECILE NIEUWENHUIZEN

LEARNING OUTCOMES

After you have studied this chapter, you should be able to:

- LO 1: Identify and explain the factors that influence the choice of a business form
- LO 2: Identify and explain the duties and the legal requirements of the various business forms
- LO 3: Explain the labour legislation that should be considered when establishing a business
- LO 4: Discuss the procedure to follow when setting up a form of business
- LO 5: Identify the factors that play a role in the choice of the location of a business
- LO 6: Identify the setting-up factors that are related to the business functions

Introduction

Thus far, you have learnt:

- how to analyse yourself critically (that is, you have determined your own strengths and weaknesses)
- how to turn a business idea into an opportunity for a new business
- how to do a viability study for the proposed business
- how to draw up a business plan.

These were covered in the evaluation and planning phases. In this final phase, we examine the practical elements of setting up a business.

> **LO 1:** Identify and explain the factors that influence the choice of a business form

6.1 Factors influencing the choice of a business form

There are many important factors to consider when choosing the correct business form. The procedure when setting up each form of business is discussed later in this chapter. Many of these are quite complicated and involve particular legal requirements and procedures. It is best to seek the advice of an accountant, auditor or attorney before you decide which form your business should take. In what follows, we will provide a brief summary of the different business forms, namely the sole proprietorship, partnership, private company, public company and close corporation. Although we have mentioned these also in Chapter 4, in this chapter we will provide a more detailed discussion of the various forms of business.

A summary of different business forms

Sole proprietorship

This is usually a small business, owned entirely by one person who is responsible for supplying the capital and running the business. All the profits belong to that person, and he/she is also responsible for all the liabilities of the business.

Partnership

This is where two or more, but not more than 20, owners combine their capital and abilities to form a business. The profits and losses are shared between the partners in an agreed ratio. The partners are liable jointly and severally for the debts of the partnership.

Private company

A private company is formed where there is at least one but not more than 50 shareholders. The name of the company must end with the words '(Proprietary) Limited' ('(Pty) Ltd'). The business is run by a board of directors elected by the shareholders. Profits are distributed among the shareholders. The liability of each shareholder is limited.

Public company

A public company must have at least seven shareholders. There is no limit to the number of shares issued by a public company. Profits are distributed between shareholders as dividends and each shareholder's liability is limited to the value of shares held. (The name of this business must end with 'Limited'.) Another difference between a public and a private company is that the general public can invest in a public company and the number of shares are unlimited.

For purposes of this book, the public company will not be included as new businesses and small businesses do not make use of the public company as a business form.

Close Corporation (CC)

The Companies Act 71 of 2008 affects an entrepreneur's choice of business structure. (The Act combines the Companies Act 61 of 1973 and the Close Corporations Act 69 of 1984, and incorporates amendments.) A primary implication of the Act is that specific attention has been paid to its provisions for small private companies. These provisions benefit the directors of a small business and replace those of a CC.

For example, one provision exempts a company from having its annual financial statements audited. However, the financial statements of a private company have to be professionally reviewed. This means that only companies exceeding a determined size with regard to employees, turnover, debt and shareholding have to be audited. If the aggregate value of the assets of a company is less than R5 million, this provision applies (Companies Regulations 28(2a), 2011:34). These provisions exist to limit cost and time constraints on smaller companies. However, because some shareholders, financiers and boards of directors insist on auditing, many smaller companies will ignore the exemption. In terms of the Companies Act 71 of 2008, from 1 May 2011, no new CCs have been permitted. However, existing CCs can continue to operate or be sold as CCs until they are changed to private companies. The CC must have at least one owner, but no more than 10. No shares are issued and a member's liability is limited unless they are guilty of negligence. The interest of each member is expressed as a percentage. (See Table 6.1 for more information.)

Table 6.1 compares the various forms of business in terms of the number of members, establishment procedures, the liability of its members, the name of the business, the legal identity of the business, provision of capital, distribution of profit, business continuity and the advantages and disadvantages of each form.

TABLE 6.1: Different forms of a business

	SOLE PROPRIETORSHIP	PARTNERSHIP	PRIVATE COMPANY	IMPLICATIONS OF COMPANIES ACT OF 2008 ON SMMEs	CLOSE CORPORATION
Number of members	Single individual owner	Two to 50	One to 50	One to 50	One to 10
Establishment procedures	Requires trade name and trade licence	Relatively simple and can be verbal or in writing.	The incorporation of a company requires certain prescribed documents to be submitted to the Companies and Intellectual Property Commission (CIPC). The CIPC then registers the company and the company then becomes a legal entity. See www.cipc.co.za for detailed information.	The Act makes provision for new categories of companies, new provisions for minority shareholders and new guidelines for financial statements.	Must be registered by the Registrar of Close Corporations with a written document giving an accounting officer permission to act in this capacity. This is relevant only for existing CCs as no new CCs can be registered.
Liability of members	The owner is personally liable for losses.	The partners are liable jointly and severally for the debts of the partnership.	Limited to paying up their share capital in the company in full.	Provision is made for companies of limited liability where owners of such companies will be protected from personal liability for business debts.	Limited liability for members. However, sometimes members can be personally liable to the corporation for their conduct.
Name of business	No restrictions as long as it is legal.	No restrictions as long as it is legal.	The name must end with the words '(Proprietary) Limited'/(Pty) Ltd'.	The name must end with the words '(Proprietary) Limited'/'(Pty) Ltd'.	The name must end with the letters CC.

	SOLE PROPRIETORSHIP	PARTNERSHIP	PRIVATE COMPANY	IMPLICATIONS OF COMPANIES ACT OF 2008 ON SMMEs	CLOSE CORPORATION
Legal entity	This business is not a legal entity. The owner is the legal person	Not a legal entity.	Has a legal personality and the assets and liabilities of the company are therefore completely separate from those of the shareholders.	Has a legal personality and the assets and liabilities of the company are therefore completely separate from those of the shareholders.	Has a legal personality and its assets and liabilities are its own.
Provision of capital	The owner is responsible for supplying all the capital.	The partners are responsible for supplying all the capital. Their creditworthiness makes it easier to obtain capital.	Capital is generated by making shares available to the shareholders. The general public cannot subscribe to the shares.	Capital is generated by making shares available to the shareholders. The general public cannot subscribe to the shares.	No shareholders; only members, who are responsible for supplying the capital.
Distribution of profits	The owner is entitled to all profits.	The profits are shared among the partners in an agreed ratio.	Profits are distributed among shareholders in the form of dividends declared on the number or value of shares held by each shareholder.	Profits are distributed among shareholders in the form of dividends declared on the number or value of shares held by each shareholder.	The members each have an interest in the business expressed as a percentage. Profitsare divided according to this percentage.
Continuity	Depends on the owner.	Partnership is dissolved on the death, resignation or insolvency of a partner.	The life is indefinite except when it is liquidated.	The life is indefinite except when it is liquidated.	It exists independently of its members.

	SOLE PROPRIETORSHIP	PARTNERSHIP	PRIVATE COMPANY	IMPLICATIONS OF COMPANIES ACT OF 2008 ON SMMEs	CLOSE CORPORATION
Disadvantages	Personally responsible for all debts, and liability is unlimited. The owner must supply all the capital. No continuity. Limited knowledge of owner.	Partners have a personal and unlimited liability for the debts of the partnership. Lack of continuity. Problems can arise if partners disagree on the management of the business. Irregularities can occur because it is not necessary to audit the financial statements of the partnership. A partner's conduct can be binding on the partnership even if other partners disagree.	Various additional costs to be paid. Compulsory disclosure of statements and constitution. The company's affairs are known to everyone, including its competitors. Detailed provisions regarding the establishment and management of the company. Employees who do not have shares in the company will not necessarily show the same interest in the company as the owner.	As soon as the company reaches a size as determined by the Companies Act of 2008, the requirements for low-turnover SMMEs are the same as for other private companies.	Each member can act on behalf of the CC and participate in its management. Selling a member's interest requires approval by all the other members. Limitation to expand due to limitation of 10 natural persons. Certain dealings can lead to personal responsibilities. Members' limited liability for the debts can make it difficult for the CC to obtain credit.

Source: Benade, Henning, du Plessis, Delport, de Koker and Pretorius, 2008

Note: Information on close corporations (CCs) is included as there are still many CCs doing business.

6.1.1 The nature of the product or service

The nature of your product, and the complexity of its development, manufacture and marketing, will determine the most suitable business form. For example, a business manufacturing security gates requires the involvement of one or two owners, staffing by a few employees, possibly a garage used as a workshop and a minimum of equipment. For this type of business, a sole proprietorship or partnership would be adequate. If, however, you set up a factory to manufacture remote-controlled gates and doors for residential and industrial use, you should consider a different business form: a higher turnover and sophisticated business venture might require a private company structure.

6.1.2 Legal liability of owners

A close corporation and a private company have specific legal personalities, while the sole proprietor and the partnership do not. 'Legal personality' means that the sole proprietor and members of a partnership are usually personally responsible for the tax and debt obligations, and the commitments of the business. Shareholders of companies and members of close corporations have limited liability for commitments of the particular business form. The person can therefore be held responsible, to a limited extent, for the commitments of the company or close corporation.

6.1.3 The business form and the effect of taxation on it

In many cases, the effect of income tax determines the choice of business form. (Tax policy changes frequently; changes are announced in the annual budget by the Minister of Finance.) The tax rate for companies and close corporations is 27% for years of assessment ending on or after 31 March 2023.

A simplified tax on turnover has been implemented for micro businesses. According to SARS (www.sars.gov.za), turnover tax is a simplified tax system for small businesses with a qualifying turnover of not more than R1 million per annum. It is a tax based on the taxable turnover of a business and is available to sole proprietors (individuals), partnerships, close corporations, companies and co-operatives. Turnover tax takes the place of VAT (in the instance that you have not decided to elect back into the VAT system), provisional tax, income tax, capital gains tax, secondary tax on companies (STC) and dividends tax. So qualifying businesses pay a single tax instead of various other taxes. It is elective, so you choose whether to participate.

There are special turnover tax rates for micro businesses as indicated in Table 6.2. Tax rates can change on an annual basis as announced by SARS through the treasury.

TABLE 6.2: Turnover tax for micro businesses
Years of assessment ending on any date between 1 March 2022 and 28 February 2023

TAXABLE TURNOVER (R)	RATE OF TAX (R)
1–335 000	0%
335 001–500 000	1% of taxable turnover above 335 000
500 001–750 000	1 650 + 2% of taxable turnover above 500 000
750 001 and above	6 650 + 3% of taxable turnover above 750 000

Source: SARS (2022)

These rates are for a year and can change annually or during the course of a year according to the announcement of the Minister of Finance.

6.1.4 Specific legal requirements

You must be aware of legal requirements for the various business forms. In the case of a company, a Memorandum of Incorporation must be registered with the Companies and Intellectual Property Commission (CIPC), and financial statements must be drawn up and approved annually by a chartered accountant. As mentioned previously, and according to the Companies Act 71 of 2008, as amended in 2011, audited statements might not be necessary for low-turnover SMMEs.

Certain businesses, such as restaurants, must renew their licences annually, for example where health inspectors have to make annual inspections. These are just a few examples of the legal requirements to which you should pay attention.

It is important to collect as much information as possible to determine the most suitable form for your proposed business. You can find information by reading books or making use of experts – attorneys, auditors or business consultants. Due to the legal requirements, it is recommended that an attorney or auditor be approached for the establishment of a private company. Before a new company can be registered, an accounting officer should be appointed.

LO 2: Identify and explain the duties and legal requirements of the various business forms

6.2 The duties and legal requirements of business forms

The duties and legal requirements that apply to all business forms include the following:

- the person operating the business must have full legal capacity
- the type of economic activity that will be undertaken must be stated
- the name of the business must be accepted
- the registration of patents, trademarks and designs must be carried out
- products testing must take place
- licensing must be done.

The business must be registered with:

- the South African Revenue Service
- the Commissioner for Unemployment Insurance
- the Workmen's Compensation Commissioner
- the relevant local authority
- the Department of Trade and Industry.

The business must comply with the following legislation:

- general industrial and commercial legislation
- the Occupational Health and Safety Act 85 of 1993.

Each of these requirements is briefly discussed below. The relevant bodies can provide the information you need.

6.2.1 Full legal capacity

Full legal capacity means that the person who runs the business must be solvent: that is, they must be able to pay their suppliers. An insolvent person or a person under judicial management may not set up a business. The risk involved in entrepreneurship can cause an entrepreneur to lose everything; those who have been legally declared insolvent are prohibited from running a business, until they have been rehabilitated by a court.

6.2.2 The type of economic activity

There are different municipal and legal requirements for different types of businesses. For example, the health requirements for a restaurant, bakery or delicatessen differ from those that apply to an insurance broker, bottle store or construction company. Find out which legal obligations you have to fulfil from your local municipality or licensing authority.

6.2.3 Naming the business

The law governing business names limits choice. The trading name of a business must be approved to protect existing businesses and avoid duplication. Company names must be approved by the CIPC. Choice of a name must comply with the requirements of the Business Names Act 27 of 1960. (Proprietary) Limited/ (Eiendoms) Beperk or (Pty) Ltd/(Edms) Bpk must appear at the end of the name of a private company (see Table 6.1). Name reservation is not mandatory, and the name reservation process is part of the company registration process. However, if a company name is rejected, the registration number becomes the name of the company.

6.2.4 Registration of patents, trademarks and designs

Anyone can patent a unique product, service, trademark or design. Registration of such a patent is performed by a patents attorney. An annual registration fee is payable after three years so that the registered patent does not expire.

There is a general impression that the cost of registering a patent is restrictive. In South Africa, this cost can be less than R20 000 (this could rise with increasing technical complexity). Foreign patent protection will cost between R40 000 and R60 000.

It may be worth considering patenting your unique product; you would be extremely disappointed if a competitor saw the value in your product and beat you to the patent office.

Trademarks can be registered at the Trademarks Office in Pretoria. For example, a design giving exclusive rights to form and colour combinations can be registered with the Designs Office. Registered trademarks are valid for 10 years, then a trademark can be renewed.

6.2.5 Testing

Products can be tested by the South African Bureau of Standards (SABS). Some companies add a clause to contracts specifying that products must be manufactured in accordance with SABS specifications.

6.2.6 Licensing

The main purpose of the Business Act 71 of 1991 is to ensure deregulation; in other words, minimise regulations and thus make it easier to establish a business. Approach the local authority to find out the rules and regulations that govern licensing in your area and for your type of business. Licences and permits required can be, for example, a liquor licence, health licence, food acceptability certificate, music usage licence and public driver's permit.

6.2.7   Registration with the South African Revenue Service

You must register your new business with the South African Revenue Service (SARS) and you must pay tax as an employer and taxpayer as well as on added value (VAT).

- **As employer:** The business must collect tax from the employees and pay it to SARS, for example SITE (Standard Income Tax on Employees) and PAYE (Pay As You Earn).

- **As taxpayer:** The business or the owner (depending on the type of business under discussion) must annually pay tax on net annual income. Businesses make provision for income tax by paying provisional tax.

- **Value-added tax (VAT):** Businesses that have an annual turnover of more than R1 million must register with SARS for payment of VAT. However, registration is voluntary for businesses making taxable income between R50 000 and R1 million. You must obtain information about the calculation and payment of VAT before setting up a business. Thorough planning and administration of the business can help you avoid fines and other problems.

IMPORTANT INFORMATION

Value-added tax is based on the following principles:

- VAT must be included in the selling price of your product or service and paid by your customers. The business therefore receives VAT on sales.

- When a business manufactures products and/or services, the business pays for raw materials and necessary materials, products and services. The business therefore pays VAT on purchases.

- The difference between the VAT that has been paid and the VAT collected must be paid monthly by the business to SARS, or claimed back.

Consult an accountant or the local SARS office for information on the registration of employees, provision for paying income tax and the payment of and claiming for VAT. These consultants can be reached at www.sars.gov.za.

You may also want to read the Tax Guide for Small Businesses on this website.

6.2.8   Registration for unemployment insurance

An employer is obliged by the Unemployment Insurance Act 30 of 1966 to make contributions to the Unemployment Insurance Fund. Employees in lower income groups qualify in terms of this law for payment of unemployment insurance by the employer. When employees resign, are dismissed or take maternity leave, they are assured of a monthly income for a certain number of months.

6.2.9   Registration with the Workmen's Compensation Commissioner

Registration is compulsory in terms of the Compensation for Occupational Injuries and Diseases Act 130 of 1993. Employees in a particular income group are compensated if, as a result of accident or injury, they can no longer earn an income. Employers pay the Workmen's Compensation Commissioner an annual amount calculated according to the total income of the employees.

EXAMPLE 6.1

A business must register as an employer with the Workmen's Compensation Commissioner within 14 days of commencing business.

6.2.10 Registration with local authorities

Businesses may have to pay service and turnover levies to the local authorities. The service levy is a percentage of the amount that is paid in salaries and wages, and the turnover levy is a percentage of the turnover of the business.

6.2.11 Registration with the Department of Trade and Industry

A new manufacturing business must register with the Department of Trade and Industry (dti). Businesses that require import permits are also obliged to register with the dti.

6.2.12 General industrial and commercial legislation

Businesses must comply with the applicable industrial legislation, for example the Occupational Health and Safety Act 85 of 1993 that provides guidelines on the duties and responsibilities of employers, employees and others about health and safety compliance in a business. The Basic Conditions of Employment Act 75 of 1997 prescribes minimum wages in cases where industrial agreements do not exist. The Consumer Protection Act 68 of 2008 (CPA) is aimed at preventing exploitation of consumers and ensuring fair business.

The long list of obligations and legal requirements can be discouraging. However, remember that registrations are mostly done only once, and that the contact people at the relevant offices are usually experts with all necessary information at their disposal.

6.2.13 Promotion of Access to Information Act (PAIA)

This Act protects the right of access to any information that the state or another person has and that is required for the exercise or protection of any rights.

6.2.14 Protection of Personal Information (PoPI) Act

The PoPI Act 4 of 2013 protects any personal information which is processed by both private and public bodies such as individuals, businesses and the government. SMMEs that collect, store and otherwise modify or use information are responsible under PoPI. SMMEs must comply with the laws governing the processing of personal information. Thus, 'personal information' has to be protected by all, including individuals and SMMEs.

LO 3: Explain the labour legislation that should be considered when establishing a business

6.3　Labour legislation

Most small businesses depend on employees; therefore, when you start your own business, knowing about and adhering to labour legislation is important. Labour legislation balances the powers of employers and employees, and is intended to protect both parties in the employment relationship. The legislation affecting this relationship is extensive, and there is unfortunately not enough space here to discuss all of it in detail. However, you can easily obtain the relevant Acts on the internet or by ordering the *Government Gazette* from the Government Printer in Pretoria. In this section, we will look at each Act briefly to ensure that you have a basic awareness of relevant legislation.

6.3.1　Employment contracts

In an employment contract, the employee makes services available to the employer. The employer describes the duties to be performed by the employee and they agree on a wage or salary. The employer–employee relationship comprises certain rights and obligations that must be mutually agreed to. The contract defines whether employment is for a fixed or indefinite period and there are three forms of contract:

1. written contracts　　2. verbal contracts　　3. tacit contracts.

Written contracts

A written contract specifies the duties and obligations of the employer and employee, for example:

- remuneration
- leave (annual, sick, maternity or other)
- working hours
- protection of the interests of the company (eg restraint of trade clauses)
- job title and position
- medical aid
- pension fund membership.

The Basic Conditions of Employment Act 75 of 1997 determines specific requirements for employment contracts. The Act requires that at least 20 particulars, as stipulated in section 29, must be reflected in the contract.

For detailed information, a copy or a summary of the Basic Conditions of Employment Act can be obtained from www.labour.gov.za.

Verbal contracts

Although verbal agreements between the employer and employee are binding, they are not recommended because in a dispute, judgment has to be made on the word of one person against another.

Tacit contracts

A tacit contract is not written, but reflects the past behaviours of the employer and employee. This arrangement is not advisable because the employer or the employee may interpret that behaviour differently.

EXAMPLE 6.2

A person is employed at a specific salary as a full-time employee, but because of a low workload, eventually works half-days only. The salary is not reduced. After a year the business situation changes and the employer then expects the employee to work a full day on the salary agreed to when the appointment was first made. The tacit agreement of working half-days may be considered binding by the employee, who then may dispute the employer's changed expectations of reverting to full-day work.

6.3.2 Labour Relations Act 66 of 1995

The Labour Relations Act 66 of 1995 (LRA) aims to establish co-determination in the workplace. The aim is to transform the relationship between management and labour from adversarial to co-operative, from fragmented dealings with one another to interaction, and from distributive to a more integrative approach. The complete Act can be obtained at www.labour.gov.za.

The primary objectives of the Act are to:

- regulate the fundamental rights of all South Africans
- promote collective bargaining and collective agreements
- promote participation of workers in the workplace
- promote the resolution of disputes.

Regulation of fundamental rights

- This section of the Act refers to freedom of association, which guarantees the rights of employees and employers to form or belong to a trade union or employers' organisation. They may then also participate in the lawful activities of these organisations, conduct elections and be elected as office-bearers or officials.

- Organisational rights are the right of the trade union to:
    - operate in the workplace
    - deduct trade union levies from members' wages
    - have reasonable leave for trade union activities for office-bearers during working hours
    - disclose certain information.

Employees are protected against:

- unfair dismissal (sections 185–197), which determines that employee dismissal should be for a valid reason, and follow a fair procedure
- unfair labour practice (Schedule 7, Part B), which includes promotion, demotion, discrimination and disciplining of employees
- strikes and lockouts (sections 64–77), which refers to the right of employees to strike and of employers to lock employees out.

Promotion of collective bargaining (sections 23–63)

The LRA aims to promote constructive co-operation between management and labour and includes:

- collective agreements
- agency shop agreements
- closed shop agreements
- collective bargaining beyond the workplace
- the establishment, powers and functions of bargaining councils
- statutory councils.

Promotion of worker participation (sections 78–94)

This enables workers to participate in the running of a business through negotiations, institutionalised consultation and joint decision-making.

Workplace forums can be formed only in businesses with more than 100 employees.

Promotion of dispute resolution

The Labour Relations Act promotes resolution of disputes at the business level, and also procedures and support structures for the resolution of labour disputes through conciliation, mediation and arbitration.

The Commission for Conciliation, Mediation and Arbitration (CCMA) was established in terms of section 112 of the LRA. It is independent of government, political parties, trade unions, employers, employees' organisations, trade union federations or employers' organisations.

The functions of the CCMA are to:

- resolve through conciliation any disputes between an employer and employee referred to it in terms of the LRA
- arbitrate disputes not resolved through conciliation, if the LRA and all parties involved agree
- assist in the establishment of workplace forums
- compile and publish information and statistics about its activities.

6.3.3   Basic Conditions of Employment Act 75 of 1997

This Act gives effect to the right to the fair labour practices referred to in section 23(1) of the Constitution of the Republic of South Africa, 1996. This is done by establishing and providing for the regulation of basic conditions of employment. The Basic Conditions of Employment Act provides for the right to reasonable and fair minimum conditions of employment.

The most important provisions of the Act are:

- a 45-hour working week (section 9) and procedures to achieve a 40-hour working week
- maximum overtime (section 10) of three hours a day and 10 hours a week; rate for overtime (section 10(2)) to be paid at one-and-a-half times the normal wage
- rest period (section 15) of at least 12 consecutive hours daily
- Sunday work (section 16) to be paid at double the normal rate
- special provisions and overtime rates for night work (section 17)
- paid leave (section 20(1)(a)) set at 21 consecutive days after 12 months at:
    - one day for every 17 days worked
    - one hour for every 17 hours worked
- proof of incapacity with a medical certificate (section 23)
- maternity leave (section 25) set at four months, with a possibility of the Unemployment Insurance Fund financing this leave
- paternity leave
- family responsibility leave (section 27) set at three days a year, after being employed for four months
- notice of termination (section 37)
- written particulars of employment (section 29). The Act requires that at least 20 particulars, as stipulated in section 29, must be reflected in your contract.

6.3.4 Employment Equity Act 55 of 1998

The aim of the Employment Equity Act 55 of 1998 is to eliminate unfair discrimination by providing equal opportunities, fair treatment in employment and affirmative action in appointments and promotion.

The Act prohibits discrimination against employees and job applicants on the basis of race, gender, pregnancy, marital responsibility, ethnic or social origin, sexual orientation, age, disability, HIV status, religion, conscious belief, political opinion, culture, language or birth.

Affirmative action determines that suitably qualified applicants/employees from the following designated groups should be employed/promoted:

1. black Africans

2. coloured people

3. asians

4. women

5. the disabled

6.3.5 Skills Development Act 97 of 1998

The aim of the Skills Development Act 97 of 1998 is to ensure that the education, training and development needs of employees are met by employers. Employers have to pay a Skills Development Levy of 1% of their annual wages and salaries to the National Skills Fund. When employees are trained or receive education, according to a specific percentage (up to 40% of the 1% paid) of their contribution will be paid back to the business. Only those small businesses with a total annual salary and wage bills of more than R500 000 per year are required to pay the Skills Development Levy.

6.3.6 Black economic empowerment (BEE)

The Broad-Based Black Economic Empowerment (BBBEE) Act 53 of 2003 provides a more inclusive definition of black empowerment. It includes criteria such as ownership, management and control, employment equity, skills development, affirmative procurement, enterprise development and social development. It also provides for transformation charters for the various sectors of the economy. According to the Act, all businesses, including SMMEs, must plan for and implement a basic framework for measured progress towards BEE. This is done by means of a scorecard. Strategic representation of previously disadvantaged groups, employment equity and skills development are important matters and should be taken into consideration to ensure survival in any business.

There are, however, some exemptions for micro and small enterprises in the BEE legislation, which includes exempted micro enterprises (EMEs) for micro enterprises with a turnover of less than R10 million. They can automatically qualify as empowering suppliers and their customers can claim BEE points. Exemptions are also allowed for qualifying small enterprises (QSEs). An SMME with a turnover up to R50 million per year qualifies as a QSE. There are specific requirements for white-owned QSEs, for example they should start to employ and train black employees, buy from BEE certified suppliers and support black businesses and communities. Black-owned QSEs automatically qualify as level 1 BEE suppliers, 51% black-owned QSEs automatically qualify as level 2 BEE suppliers.

LO 4: Discuss the procedure to follow when setting up each form of business

6.4   The procedure for setting up forms of business

In this section, we will look at the different procedures to follow in setting up the various forms of business.

6.4.1   The sole proprietorship and the partnership

Few legal requirements govern establishing a sole proprietorship and a partnership. The laws and regulations discussed in Section 6.3 apply to these. A partnership is formed by a written or oral agreement between partners.

6.4.2   The company

Major changes have been established in the Companies Act 71 of 2008, as discussed in this chapter and in Chapter 4. The new Act prescribes how a company should be formed. For example, registration and creation of a company is performed by the office of the CIPC in Pretoria.

The steps in setting up a company are:

- **A Memorandum of Association and Statutes/Articles must be drawn up:** A chartered accountant or an attorney can be appointed to do this. Each signatory of the Memorandum of Association receives a specified number of shares and this is recorded. (There is only one shareholder in a one-person company.) Signatories to the Memorandum also sign the Statutes.

- **The following documents and information must be submitted to the Companies and Intellectual Property Commission (CIPC) for the registration of a company:** Details of the reserved or approved name, the translation of the name or a shortened form, if applicable. As mentioned previously name reservation is no longer a separate procedure or mandatory. The registration number becomes the name of the company if the name is rejected.

- Two copies of the Memorandum of Association and Statutes that have been signed as prescribed, in addition to the original Memorandum of Association and Statutes.
- Information concerning the location of the registered office and postal address (also a form of the Companies Act).
- For companies with higher turnovers, written acceptance by a chartered accountant that they are prepared to audit the annual financial statements.
- A fixed amount of annual duty should accompany the application at registration.
- Proof that the registration fee has been paid.
- A company can be registered electronically with the CIPC.

The CIPC provides proof that the company has been registered at CIPC and is therefore a legal entity.

6.4.3   The close corporation

As from 1 May 2011 there is no provision for the registration of new close corporations.

LO 5: Identify the factors that play a role in the choice of the location of a business

6.5   Factors that play a role in the choice of location

Many factors affect the choice of a suitable location for your business. It is a good idea to read widely on the topic, make enquiries and ask experts for advice.

Consider the following:
- **The market:** This is especially important for a trading enterprise which must be visible and accessible to its market.
- **Access to raw materials:** This particularly affects manufacturing businesses. You should consider whether it is more important to be close to the market or close to raw materials. The type of raw materials and the type of final product will determine this choice. For example, the factory of a roof sheeting manufacturer should be built near a power station to reduce the transport costs of coal ash.
- **Human resources/labour:** Ensure that you will be able to employ suitable staff in your area.
- **Costs:** Compare the cost of renting or buying premises in different locations and compare these with your competitor's costs. (Cheapest is not always best.)

- **Climate:** An example that best illustrates this point would be a business that produces leather outfits for men and women. This type of business would no doubt sell more outfits if located in Cape Town (which has cold and wet winters) than Durban (where temperatures remain moderate even during the winter).

- **Regional incentive programmes:** To encourage development in particular regions or industries, the government operates industrial incentive schemes. These provide, for example, financing for building factories in certain areas, reduced taxation for a specific period, grants for businesses in the tourism industry and so on. Contact the Department of Trade and Industry and your local authorities for more information.

- **Services:** Check the availability of services such as public transport, water supply, parking space, electricity and support services from other businesses in the area that you are considering.

- **Personal and social considerations:** These are often the most important factors in choosing a location. Consider whether the premises are close enough to where you and your staff live to make the location convenient for all of you.

Finally, remember that location will have a huge influence on competitiveness. Conduct thorough market research before signing a rental or purchase agreement – and seriously consider seeking professional advice from an attorney before signing.

Remember you do not have to accept the first set of terms offered by the estate agent or owner of the premises. It is possible to negotiate a rental agreement that will be better for the business. Here you should be informed of your rights as in the Consumer Protection Act 68 of 2008.

LO 6: Identify the setting-up factors that are related to the business functions

6.6　Setting-up factors that are related to the business functions

A large variety of activities occur within a small business in the process of providing goods and/or services. These activities can be systematically divided into smaller groups by placing similar activities together. Each group of activities is called a function. We can identify eight interdependent ones:

1. Marketing is responsible for all activities related to supplying the consumer with the products or services provided by the business.

2. Public relations is the promotion of a positive impression of the business in the external environment.

3. Information and record keeping involves control of information systems to ensure that information is obtained, processed and made available to management.

4. Finance involves budgeting and the effective application and use of funds.

5. Human resources includes the effective use of employees as well as their recruitment, development, retention and morale.

6. Purchasing is responsible for the timely purchasing of goods and services at the right price, and of the required quality and quantity from suppliers.

7. Operations is responsible for transforming inputs such as raw materials, labour and finance into outputs – the products or services that the business offers.

8. General management primarily consists of the activities of planning, organising, leading and control. These include supporting the other functions in achieving their objectives.

Together, the eight functions represent all the activities performed in a typical, mature business. In subsequent sections we take a look at what must be done in each function when a business is set up. Bear in mind that performances overlap.

6.6.1 The marketing function

As you saw in the example of the business plan in Chapter 5, it is important to plan your marketing and its campaigns. Consider the target market, the variety of products and/or services to be offered, their price, how they will be distributed and when. This is the core of the marketing plan (see Figure 6.1).

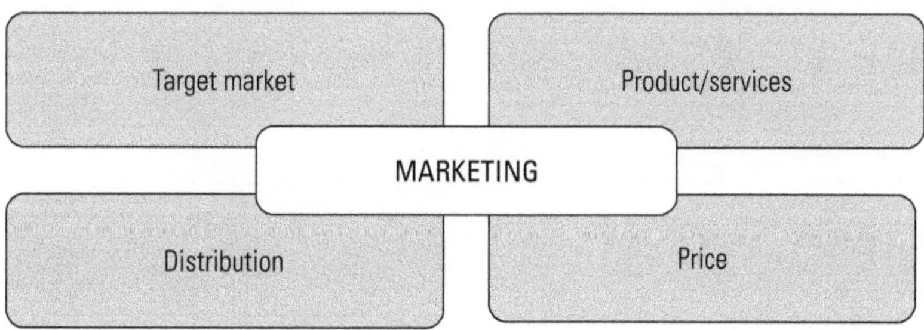

FIGURE 6.1: The core of the marketing plan

The marketing plan therefore answers the following questions:

- Where are we now?
- Where do we want to be?
- How do we get there?
- How do we exercise control?

Consumer Protection Act 68 of 2008

You must also be sure that the business can and will deliver what your marketing promises. Consumers are protected by provisions in the Consumer Protection Act that include:

- the right to fair marketing
- the right to return goods and get refunds
- the right of a six-month warranty on all products bought
- strict liability, giving the consumer the right to sue if goods cause injury or damage.

Name, logo and motto

By this stage you will have chosen a name for your business and a motto. (The motto is a brief description that encapsulates the ethos or ideals of your business in a few words.)

EXAMPLE 6.3

Avis (the car rental company) uses the motto 'We try harder'. Nike's motto is 'Just do it' and De Beers: 'A diamond is forever'.

Once you have the name (and possibly registered it with the CIPC), you should not change it because as your product or service becomes associated with that name, it becomes a valuable marketing tool. Any change of name or change of directors must be registered with the CIPC.

EXAMPLE 6.4

It is also a good idea to have a logo that illustrates the name and mission statement of your business. You can use it and possibly any elements of your mission statement on your letterheads, business cards, invoices and any other business stationery.

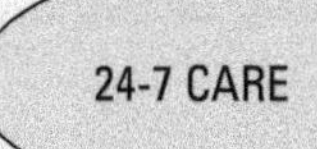

EXAMPLE 6.5

The abbreviations CC or (Pty) Ltd and the company registration number must always appear on stationery.

The names of members (for a CC) and directors (for a (Pty) Ltd) must also appear on stationery.

Form of communication

Consider the best form of communication in marketing your business. Consider where and how your competitors advertise, and how they market their products. Then consider the same advertising channels, but remember to distinguish your advertisements from those of competitors in a significant way. For the small business, personal sales are an important site method of communication where prospective customers are contacted personally or by word of mouth; and where satisfied customers recommend the business to networks of friends, family and acquaintances.

The internet is one of the foremost ways to advertise your business. A web page designed for your business is also a relatively cost-effective way of advertising a new business.

The cost of advertising is high; therefore, it is a good idea to develop a method of monitoring the results of each advertisement. In this way you can determine the cost-effectiveness of each method.

EXAMPLE 6.6

A person gives quotations for garden services by appointment. When prospective customers call to make the appointment, find out how they heard of your business. In this way, the hit rate on each advertisement can be established.

Note the number of sales that each advertisement generates. Remember that on certain days of the week your customers may respond more easily to an advertisement.

EXAMPLE 6.7

Job seekers react more to advertisements at certain times of the year. Thus, an employment agency will advertise positions in the local or a national newspaper at the beginning of the year rather than before the December holidays, or during the term rather than during holidays or at long weekends. And restaurants will focus their advertising on periods when their customers are more likely to dine out – over weekends and around month-end pay days when prospective customers will be more likely to have money available for entertainment.

6.6.2 The public relations function

Try as far as possible to use public relations to promote the image of your business. In public relations the image of the business as a whole is important. Its goals include creating goodwill, understanding, acceptance and co-operation with those affected or likely to be affected by the business. (Do not confuse this with marketing, which is responsible for promoting specific products or services.)

Here are some hints about public relations:

- Use acquaintances and friends who can make your business known; in other words, use your network of people and friends (the process known as 'networking').
- Invite journalists from the local newspaper to the opening of the business.
- If the press cannot attend, write the article yourself and send photographs with it for publication.
- Ask for an advertorial, promotional article or article to be written about your business when you are placing advertisements in a publication.

It is important to use creative and even alternative methods of publicity to make your business known and to distinguish it from similar businesses.

EXAMPLE 6.8

The following is a good example of successful public relations.

Bolonois, a lifestyle village for people over the age of 60, invited special guests and the press to an art exhibition and cheese-and-wine function to market the village and its service offerings. They publicised the event by involving an estate agent, who invited clients that might be interested in buying a property in a village, and by sending personal invitations to the media, prospective clients, their friends and colleagues.

It was a sophisticated and free function with art by various artists for sale, and aimed at the likely buyers. The launch was personal and the refreshments and the service excellent: they gave a foretaste of the quality of Belenois' service.

The owners relied on personal recommendations as their primary medium of marketing. After the function, a few articles were published, thus many more became aware of Belenois, with the result that a strongly representative group of the target market now buys or recommends that their friends and family buy property at Belenois or send their loved ones for mid- or frail-care to its facilities.

Testimonials from satisfied clients are also excellent forms of public relations. Ensure that clients have the opportunity to give feedback on their experience with your business, for example by filling out a 'customer comments section' on your web page.

Relevant organisations and associations can be beneficial for promoting your business. Local chambers of commerce as well as business and sports clubs are just a few examples of where valuable contacts can be built up.

6.6.3   The information and record systems function

From the first day your business starts trading, records of relevant information must be kept. It is important to develop an effective and user-friendly record-keeping system.

Some examples and requirements of record-keeping systems are:

- a system for keeping information about clients
- an accounting system that you understand and which is simple and effective
- an effective stock control system
- a system for the control of cash
- a system for keeping records of marketing, enquiries and sales
- a record of turnover and profit for tax purposes and, among others, for levies to local authorities.

The kind of information you must record determines which filing systems, electronically or in a cloud, are most effective. Customer specifications and documentation including information sheets, documents and files will warrant a file for each client, stored alphabetically in a steel cabinet or electronically/in a cloud. A town and regional planner, for example, would open a file for each project/client and keep everything, such as maps and plans relating to that job, in it. On the other hand, if you only need to store clients' personal information, a card system will be sufficient. (A hairdresser or beautician might use such a card system.) Equally, recording and storing can be electronic, with files and folders for different clients.

Many computer programs for information management and filing are available, ranging from Microsoft Office and Microsoft-based programs to specialist programs like the Sage VIP payroll programs for businesses. Information of most businesses can be computerised, although some functions might not be computerised, such as personal files of employees.

6.6.4   The financial function

When you conducted your viability study (discussed in Chapter 4), you would have determined:

- what capital is required to set up the business
- how the capital requirement will be financed.

Financing your business

Financing institutions generally expect borrowers to show their commitment to their business by investing in it, requiring a certain amount of own investment to show that you, as the entrepreneur, are committed to the business and motivated. Before seeking bank finance, you should use some personal funds for a portion of the initial capital.

Ensure that you obtain the right finance for your requirements.

EXAMPLE 6.9

For a fixed asset such as a hotel, you would probably need a large amount of money to supplement your own investment. For this, you would need long-term financing.

For smaller and less costly assets such as computer equipment, you would need only short-term financing. It is desirable to pay off computer equipment quickly, because technology quickly becomes outdated.

Different financial institutions specialise in specific areas. Financial institutions such as Business Partners, the small, medium and micro enterprise (SMME) sections of banks, and development corporations (such as Ithala in KwaZulu-Natal) can provide financing for SMMEs. Financing ranges from direct loans to incentive schemes, and programmes can be adapted to your requirements. In addition, the Small Enterprise Finance Agency (Sefa) (www.sefa.org.za) provides access to survivalist, micro, small and medium businesses. This is done through intermediaries as well as their nine offices in all the country's provinces. Sefa provides credit guarantees to SMMEs and supports financial intermediaries such as banks to assist SMMEs.

EXAMPLE 6.10

Funders can also be approached. For example, Acorn Technologies, a government-funded incubator for companies in the life science arena, has developed a website which aims to link suitable investors with entrepreneurs or companies that need start-up or expansion financing. See the various websites, including https://www.spartan.co.za/sme-finance, for more information and extensive and searchable databases of fund providers in South Africa, including their investment criteria and contact details.

For more information on financing your business and related matters, such as start-ups, building and growing your business, incentive schemes, tender opportunities and new business opportunities, the website of the Small Enterprise Development Agency (Seda), www.seda.org.za, covers everything of interest to the small business entrepreneur.

Managing your finances

You should consider the following points:

- **Develop a basic accounting system:** This need not be complicated, but it must suit your business and be understandable.

- **Appoint an external bookkeeper or accountant:** Do this if you do not wish, or are not able, to handle the bookkeeping yourself. The cost of this service will be worth it. A small business can sometimes share an accountant with other businesses. A bookkeeper will need to spend one or two days a week or month to do your accounts.

- **Draw up specific cash budgets (as discussed in Chapter 4):** This is part of the planning for the next period. Adjust the budgets if necessary. Budgets are important, because they indicate when cash will be available and when cash-flow problems may be experienced. They are essential for planning and useful in controlling business activities.

- **Maintain a good relationship with your bank:** To obtain additional capital and ensure a helpful attitude on the part of the bank manager or personal banker, it is important to meet your obligations punctually. If, for some reason or other, this is not possible, explain the situation to the bank manager so that alternative arrangements can be made. A bank manager who is kept informed is better able to help you and your business.

- **Insurance:** Make provision for the insurance of stock, vehicles, contents of your office, contracts, equipment, buildings, etc.

- **Establish creditworthiness:** If you sell on credit, make sure you check the creditworthiness of your customers. This can be done by asking customers to supply trade references and banking details. Information can also be bought from credit bureaus. Before supplying goods on credit, establish the terms on which credit will be granted (eg 60 days) and stick to them.

- **Keep up to date with economic affairs:** Read financial magazines and the business section of the newspaper. It is particularly important to be aware of economic factors such as interest rates and inflation.

6.6.5 Human resources function

To plan your staffing requirements and ensure that your appointments are sound, consider the following suggestions:

- Draw up a list of all the tasks that must be performed in the business.

- Group tasks so that tasks that can be performed by a specific person. This combination of tasks becomes the job description.

- Determine what qualifications and skills the person must have to perform the tasks. These are the job specifications of the appointment.

- Then recruit the right people. This involves:
  - placing an advertisement, conducting interviews and reference-checking yourself
  - using a recruitment agency (they charge a fee that usually ranges from 7 to 15% of an appointment's annual salary)
  - seek recommendations from staff at training organisations (schools, technical colleges or tertiary institutions).
- When you search for people with specific personal characteristics and attributes for a demanding or specialised position it is also good to do psychometric evaluation through an industrial psychologist. This helps to determine whether the candidate has the attributes required.

Once you have found the right candidate, draw up an employment contract. (The employment contract is discussed in section 6.3.1.) Make sure you give your new employee a clear, written job description when you sign the employment contract together.

IMPORTANT INFORMATION

Think carefully before appointing family or friends, as this has many pitfalls. You may be tempted to make such an appointment because it is the quickest or easiest method, or to help a friend or family member, or because the person has a specific characteristic that might benefit the business.

However, doing this means that you do not compare the person with other suitable candidates for the post. Examples of complications include:

- the appointed person does not have the necessary skills or qualifications
- personal and working relationships differ
- friction can arise and harm the business
- the appointed person could become jealous of you, the employer
- family appointments and promotions can make other employees jealous
- friction could arise between other family members and friends.

6.6.6 The purchasing function

Find out about trade and speciality shows. You can make purchases at shows, and obtain information about innovations and product developments in your area of business. And you can market your products at shows, virtual and in-person.

EXAMPLE 6.11

SARCDA Trade Exhibitions holds an annual show where wholesalers in gifts, household goods, décor, design, toys and general retail products display their products to retailers and service providers. Buyers view a large variety of products under one roof and can place orders with wholesalers. Similar shows exist for the catering, jewellery, construction, beauty, interior decorating, antique collectors and fashion industries. These shows are now often a combination of an actual, live show as well as virtual options.

Consider the following points when setting up your purchasing function:

- Negotiate with suppliers for better prices for cash, to obtain products on consignment or for 30-day accounts. The financial planning of the business will determine the most favourable payment method for purchases.

- Compare suppliers not only in terms of price but also in terms of the quality and their services (eg do they deliver and install?).

- Keep stock to a minimum and control it properly: carrying stock costs money. The 'just-in-time' (JIT) system is an effective stock-control system that was originally developed in Japan. Stock is delivered just in time to limit the costs of carrying stock. However, for sound customer service, it is essential to have sufficient stock on hand and situations caused by the Covid-19 pandemic proved that it is not always the best idea to keep minimal stock.

- Be careful not to become too dependent on a single supplier. This can cause problems when this supplier is out of stock, prices become too high or service deteriorates. Find and use alternative suppliers to maintain good service.

- There is no harm in creating price and service competition between your suppliers by letting them know that they are not your sole providers. Obtain price lists, information on discounts and catalogues from various suppliers.

- Cultivate good relationships with suppliers. This ensures better service and is especially important when, for instance, raw materials are in short supply, when your supplier may give you preferential treatment.

6.6.7 The operational function

Consider some or all of the following:

- Meticulously planned machinery and other equipment supplies and maintenance controls capital investment and best use. Having adequate, reliable equipment ensures timely production or service.

- Train labour to ensure the correct use of equipment.

- Secure expert design and knowledgeable layout of production facilities.
- Cost control ensures a profitable operation.
- Inspections and operational procedures are control measures.
- Manage production time. Clients' orders should be executed as agreed and this requires careful planning of equipment and labour use.
- Bottlenecks often occur where specialised labour and expensive equipment are involved. Sound planning is essential to prevent bottlenecks and help ensure that deliveries can be made on time.
- Outsourcing certain functions in the production process is an option to:
  - Eliminate specific bottlenecks. A building contractor will use subcontractors – for example, for carpentry – when their own employees are engaged or the contractor does not have his own specialised teams such as carpenters and plumbers.
  - Postpone purchase of expensive equipment. A business that manufactures doors and windows with aluminium frames will initially buy the door handles and window catches from a supplier. When sufficient profit has been made, it can purchase the equipment for making them.
  - Ensure availability of labour. A nursery will refer clients who are interested in a professionally designed garden to an independent, expert landscape architect. The nursery can offer this service without having to bear the costs of specialist service. It can even make an agreement with the landscape architect to buy all the plants and supplies from the nursery.

6.6.8 The general management function

As an entrepreneur, you will be the manager of your business during its establishment stage. You will therefore be responsible for:

- formulating goals for the business
- encouraging staff to achieve these
- performing the management functions of planning, organising, leading and controlling.

As manager, you will also be responsible for effectively co-ordinating business functions.

You may appoint an outside person to perform a specific function, such as a marketing manager who would be responsible for the entire marketing function on a part-time basis. You may also wish to outsource some functions.

EXAMPLE 6.12

An interior decorator outsources the operations function, having different contractors manufacture the products such as curtains, couches and chairs for clients. The overall responsibility for management, however, remains with the decorator, who must ensure that the business functions as a profitable entity.

If you do not have the skills or resources to perform functions requiring particular, specialised or professional skills, outsourcing may be necessary. It ensures cost-effectiveness and makes effective management possible.

It is also a management function to determine the optimal operating capacity of the business. A business reaches its optimal operating capacity when inputs, labour and/or production factors are used to the maximum to ensure the maximum output. When a new business is established, it seldom functions at full capacity from the start because the business has fewer orders or clients, thus less demand. The business possibly starts below or at break-even point, with the prospect of obtaining more business to allow it to function optimally. That stage will ensure increased profits. Remember, however, that the availability of specific equipment and labour is crucial to the production of a particular quantity of products.

There may come a time when demand exceeds maximum possible capacity and additional costs may be necessary to meet the new demand, but it may not be possible to provide for just a single demand increase.

Suppose demand for a product rises by 100 units. The equipment for manufacturing the additional units costs R12 000. This expenditure, however, causes the production capacity to increase beyond immediate need: an additional 800 units can be manufactured. At this point, a new break-even point must be calculated to determine whether it is worthwhile raising production capacity and risking the costs of excess capacity. If the continued demand does not justify the purchase of additional equipment, there are alternative methods of increasing output. These may be:

- overtime
- producing during quiet periods for stock build-up
- contracting out certain functions or processes
- contracting out manufacturing of specific quantities of products
- hiring equipment
- appointing temporary labour and/or labour on contract.

Thus, you should ensure that the possible expansion of your business will result in a real increase in income. The expense of increased capacity should not exceed the anticipated income resulting from expanded capacity. In certain cases, such as when a constant increase in demand is expected, higher expenses than income may be acceptable at first. Then, it is important that realistic forecasts and planning occurs to ensure long-term profitability.

Another managerial responsibility is to draw up considered contracts between the business and relevant parties:

- employees
- landlords
- clients.

Here as elsewhere, clear and unambiguous contracts prevent financial, personal and even legal conflicts.

6.7　Summary

Growth changes businesses. When a new business is established, the set-up and establishment factors are not the same for all businesses. The entrepreneur has to determine critical success factors and in planning should concentrate on these. Remember that the emphasis of the business often shifts and that growth creates new and different demands on the entrepreneur. A business that employed few or no staff will eventually have to appoint more; an entrepreneur who at first does their own marketing may later have to use a marketing specialist. The entrepreneur must therefore note the critical success factors in the setting-up stage, but be aware that the situation is not static. Change comes rapidly; it is important to make provision for it timeously to ensure competitiveness.

SELF-EVALUATION QUESTIONS

1. Identify the most suitable form for the business you are planning and give three reasons for your choice.

2. Discuss the procedures that you will have to follow to set up the business in this business form.

3. Briefly describe your planned business and indicate which legal registrations and requirements for licensing apply.

4. Determine the labour legislation applicable to the business that you are planning.

5. Considering the same business you are planning, list the most important factors in choice of location and indicate why each plays a role.

6. How will you manage each business function in the setting-up stage of your planned business?

REFERENCES AND FURTHER READING

Benade, ML, Henning, JJ, Du Plessis, JJ, Delport, PA, De Koker, L & Pretorius, JT. 2008. *Entrepreneurial Law*. LexisNexis: Durban.

CIPC. Companies and Intellectual Property Commission. http://www.cipc.co.za (Accessed 31 July 2018).

SARS. South African Revenue Service. https://www.sars.gov.za (Accessed 19 July 2022).

SARS. South African Revenue Service. SARS tax pocket guide. http://www.treasury.gov.za (Accessed 11 March 2022).

Legislation

Basic Conditions of Employment Act 75 of 1997.

Broad-Based Black Economic Empowerment Act 53 of 2003.

Business Act 71 of 1991.

Business Names Act 27 of 1960.

Close Corporations Act 69 of 1984.

Companies Act 61 of 1973.

Companies Act 71 of 2008.

Companies Regulations, 2011.

Compensation for Occupational Injuries and Diseases Act 130 of 1993.

Constitution of the Republic of South Africa, 1996.

Consumer Protection Act 68 of 2008.

Employment Equity Act 55 of 1998.

Labour Relations Act 66 of 1995.

Promotion of Access to Information Act 2 of 2000.

Protection of Personal Information Act 4 of 2013.

Occupational Health and Safety Act 85 of 1993.

Skills Development Act 97 of 1998.

Stamp Duties Act 77 of 1968.

Unemployment Insurance Act 30 of 1966.

Appendix

PETER'S BUSINESS (PTY) LTD
BUSINESS PLAN
January 2023

Compiled by:
Peter Mashaba
Chief Executive Officer: Peter's Business (Pty) Ltd
Mamelodi East X4435, Gauteng
Tel: 076 123 7890
Email: peter@milk.co.za
www.petersbusiness.co.za

Note:
- This document contains confidential and proprietary information belonging exclusively to Peter's Business (Pty) Ltd.
- This document does not imply an offering of shares.

Confidentiality Agreement

It is acknowledged by the undersigned that information furnished is confidential in nature, other than that in the public domain and that any disclosure or use of this information by the investor, except as provided in this agreement, may cause serious harm or damage to Peter's Business (Pty) Ltd and its owners and officers. The investor agrees that the parties will not use the information furnished for any purpose other than as stated above. At the close of negotiations, the investor will return to Peter's Business (Pty) Ltd all records, reports, documents and memoranda provided to the investor.

_______________________________________   16 January 2023
[*Signature of investor*]   [*Date*]

Rupert Learing
Managing Director: Learing & Associate Investors
[*Name, capacity and company*]

1. Executive summary

Peter Mashaba established Peter's Business in 2007 in East Mamelodi, Gauteng. His humble beginnings were as an entrepreneur buying milk from a dairy farmer close to this area and reselling it to his neighbours, from his 20 m² bedroom. A social need for different daily quantities of fresh milk led to establishing a small retail outlet and later the 200 m² Mamelodi Dairy Market, which became well known in the area.

Peter also identified and exploited the opportunity to make cheese and yoghurt as derivative products of milk. This business unit operates from a factory in Waltloo, Pretoria. It provides customised products to delicatessens and home industries in the broader Tshwane Metropolitan Area.

The business intends to increase its turnover to R4,5 million in 2023 with growth strategies, as explained in more detail in the business plan. The gross profit margin is approximately 60%.

The primary purpose of this plan is that of a planning instrument. It will be adapted to the needs of an investor in order to finance some of the medium-term growth strategies, for example the purchase of a dairy farm.

2. Business description

2.1 General description of the business

Peter's Business is a (Pty) Ltd company that was established in 2007. It initially operated as a milk reseller in the Mamelodi area. The business grew organically and diversified to include different milk packaging formats, and yoghurt and cheese. The current market expanded from the Lusaka area in Mamelodi East to include up-market delicatessens and home industries in the entire Tshwane Metropolitan Area.

The distribution structure of Peter's Business is as follows:

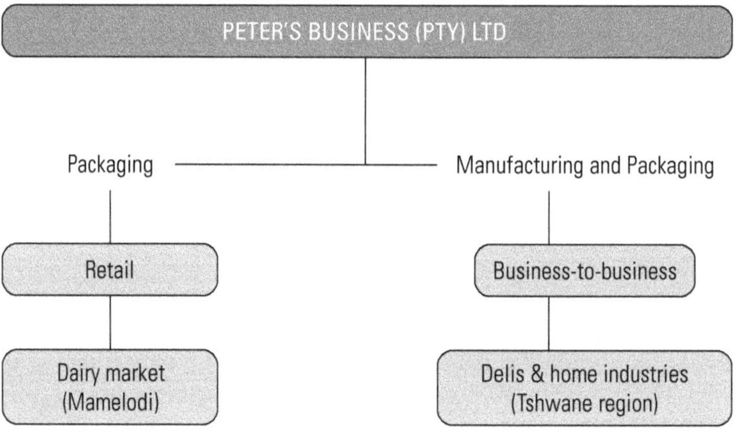

Peter's Business operates from a medium-sized manufacturing unit in the industrial area of Waltloo, Silverton (Pretoria), where all the fresh milk is received and either repackaged in smaller units (500 ml, 1 litre or 2 litre) or transformed into yoghurt and cheese products.

Peter's Business owns a dairy business that was started in 2007 and later expanded to a dairy market of approximately 200 m^2 in Mamelodi East. This retail outlet sells only fresh milk to residents in the area, either in bulk or in smaller units.

The business-to-business leg of the business entails offering yoghurt and cheese products to five delicatessens and 15 home industries in the broader Tshwane Metropolitan Area. Peter's Business intends to expand this offering to the northern parts of Johannesburg in the near future.

2.2   Industry background

The dairy branch of the industry has the following characteristics that are relevant to the retail end:

- a growing demand for healthy dairy-related products (eg no-fat and low-fat products)
- a low profit margin for the producer
- a decline in the number of producers of fresh milk
- an increase in the cost of transport for perishable products
- a big increase in consumer spending on retail goods
- a big demand for specialised dairy products (eg cheese).

2.3   Primary business goals

Short-term goals (2023–2024):

- to increase its overall turnover to R4.5 million
- to obtain two contracts for delivery of cheese and yoghurt in the northern Johannesburg region
- to buy another truck for self-delivery
- to appoint a general manager at the factory
- to identify potential dairy farms for purchase.

Medium-term goals (2024–2025):

- to increase overall turnover to R6 million per annum
- to obtain seven contracts for the delivery of cheese and yoghurt in the northern Johannesburg region
- to establish a delivery network of at least four trucks
- to expand the factory layout to 1 000 m^2

- to purchase a dairy farm (backward integration) close to the Mamelodi Dairy Market as a sole self-supplier.

Long-term goals (2025–2026):
- to increase turnover to R10 million per annum
- to become the leading BEE milk and related product provider in Gauteng.

2.4 Uniqueness of the product/service

Peter's Business aims to sell products of the highest standards. It offers the following unique services:

Mamelodi Dairy Market:
- sells fresh milk six days a week from 07:00 to 18:00 and this enables working parents and households to buy milk before or after work
- allows customers to use and reuse their own containers of any size
- provides adequate parking and enough attendants at the cash registers to serve customers and limit long queues
- provides information booklets about the health aspects of dairy products and basic recipes
- maintains a loyal customer base
- has a low-price strategy, especially for customers with own containers.

The business-to-business leg of Peter's Business:
- offers custom-made yoghurt and cheese products with unique characteristics and shapes
- ensures a continuous supply based on customer demand
- provides delivery of fresh products
- maintains good relationships with customers.

3. Marketing plan

3.1 Market research and analysis

A research survey by a private specialist into dairy products in the Mamelodi area found a huge need for fresh milk and milk products, particularly milk at a better price than available at the spaza outlets in the area. Supplying the highest quality milk is vital to the enterprise.

3.2   Target market

The market for Peter's Business is segmented into two basic target markets, served by the Mamelodi Dairy Market and the business-to-business leg of Peter's Business respectively.

The Mamelodi Dairy Market target market comprises:

- households within a 5 km radius of the outlet and on the eastern side of Mamelodi
- households of an average size of five individuals
- households with an income of between R1 500 and R5 000 per month
- households that buy milk twice a week (with an average of 2 litres per purchase)
- mainly women, who are the primary purchasers of fresh milk in this region.

The business-to-business leg of the business comprises:

- the top end of the market (high income)
- the sale of yoghurt and cheese branded as 'homemade' yoghurt and cheese
- delicatessens in the Tshwane Metropolitan Area
- home industries in the Tshwane Metropolitan Area.

3.3   Market size and market share

The current market size for the two target markets is as follows:

- Mamelodi Dairy Market: 120 000 households, of which it is believed that Peter's Business has captured 40% of the market share.
- Business-to-business: 35 delicatessens and home industries exist in the Tshwane Metropolitan Area and Peter's Business is believed to have captured a 57% share of that market.

3.4   Competition

Peter's Business operates in a highly competitive market environment and each market segment competes with the following (a detailed competitive analysis is available on request):

Mamelodi Dairy Market:
A. spaza shops (eight in the immediate market environment)
B. Checkers, approximately 7 km from the outlet
C. outside the area – indirect competition (people buying milk on their way from work).

Business-to-business:

A. large bulk suppliers (eg Makro and Jumbo), although they do not offer the same specialised products
B. dairy farms surrounding the Tshwane Metropolitan Area with more or less the same product types
C. importing companies that obtain specialised cheeses from the Netherlands and Switzerland and other regions of South Africa (although their prices are much higher).

3.5   Marketing strategy

Product strategy

The following product mix exists:

Mamelodi Dairy Market

FRESH MILK IN CONTAINERS (FULL CREAM):
500 ml plastic containers
1 litre plastic containers
2 litre plastic containers
FRESH MILK IN OWN CONTAINERS (FULL CREAM):
Any volumes between 500 ml and 5 litres

Business-to-business

YOGHURT:
300 ml plastic container – flavoured: strawberry; vanilla; chocolate
1 litre plastic container – flavoured: strawberry; vanilla; chocolate
5 litre plastic container – unflavoured

CHEESE:
200 g to 2 kg Cheddar
500 g to 2 kg Feta
200 g to 2 kg Gouda

3.6 Pricing strategy

Pricing is as follows:

Mamelodi Dairy Market

FRESH MILK IN CONTAINERS (FULL CREAM):	PRICE (R) PER UNIT:
500 ml plastic containers	5,00
1 litre plastic containers	7,00
2 litre plastic containers	10,00

FRESH MILK IN OWN CONTAINERS (FULL CREAM):	PRICE (R) PER UNIT:
Any volume between 500 ml and 5 litres	6,00/litre

Business-to-business

YOGHURT:	PRICE (R) PER UNIT:
300 ml plastic container – flavoured: strawberry; vanilla; chocolate	3,00
1 litre plastic container – flavoured: strawberry; vanilla; chocolate	11,00
5 litre plastic container – unflavoured	40,00

CHEESE:	PRICE (R) PER UNIT:
200 g to 2 kg Cheddar	80,00/kg
500 g to 2 kg Feta	110,00/kg
200 g to 2 kg Gouda	85,00/kg

3.7 Promotion strategy

Peter's Business uses the following promotion strategies:

Mamelodi Dairy Market: Currently the most effective medium of promotion for this leg of the business is 'word-of-mouth'. The Mamelodi Dairy Market is known for its quick and effective service, quality and availability of fresh milk. Community involvement is vital in promoting the business and involves younger people who are coached and trained and whose skills are developed. A 2m × 3m billboard is used as the main advertising medium and indicates the specials available every fortnight.

Business-to-business:
The promotion strategy for this business unit uses direct marketing to delicatessens and home industries.

- Peter visits each retail outlet monthly and attempts to see at least one new customer a month. The entire product line is shown and tasted, then tailored to the different needs of customers (retailers).
- Peter attends at least three trade shows a year. He links his promotion strategy to factory capacity.

3.8   Distribution strategy

Peter's Business obtains all its milk from a reliable dairy farmer close to the small town of Cullinan. This farm is approximately 8 km from the Mamelodi Dairy Market and 14 km from the Waltloo factory. (In a context of increasingly high transport costs for perishables, proximity to supplier is a business advantage.) The farmer delivers directly to the Mamelodi Dairy Market at a cost of R10 per kilometre. Peter has decided to buy a cooler truck to transfer the milk to the factory in Waltloo. This truck will also double up as a delivery vehicle for the business-to-business units. Milk delivery to the factory is daily and deliveries to the retail customers weekly, increasing during high season.

4.   Location

The Mamelodi Dairy Market and the Waltloo factory are close to the supplier (as indicated in the marketing plan) and also close to the respective target markets. Expansion on both these sites is a long-term objective of the business. Peter employs only people from the immediate community and provides training as needed.

5.   Management plan

Peter's Business has reached a point of growth where a professional management team should be appointed to extend the achievements of the founder's entrepreneurial management. (Peter currently works seven days a week for approximately 12 hours a day.)

5.1   Organisational structure

Peter therefore plans to reorganise the structure of the business to spend more time on strategic matters. This is a requirement for continued growth. The following organisational structure will be established in the short term:

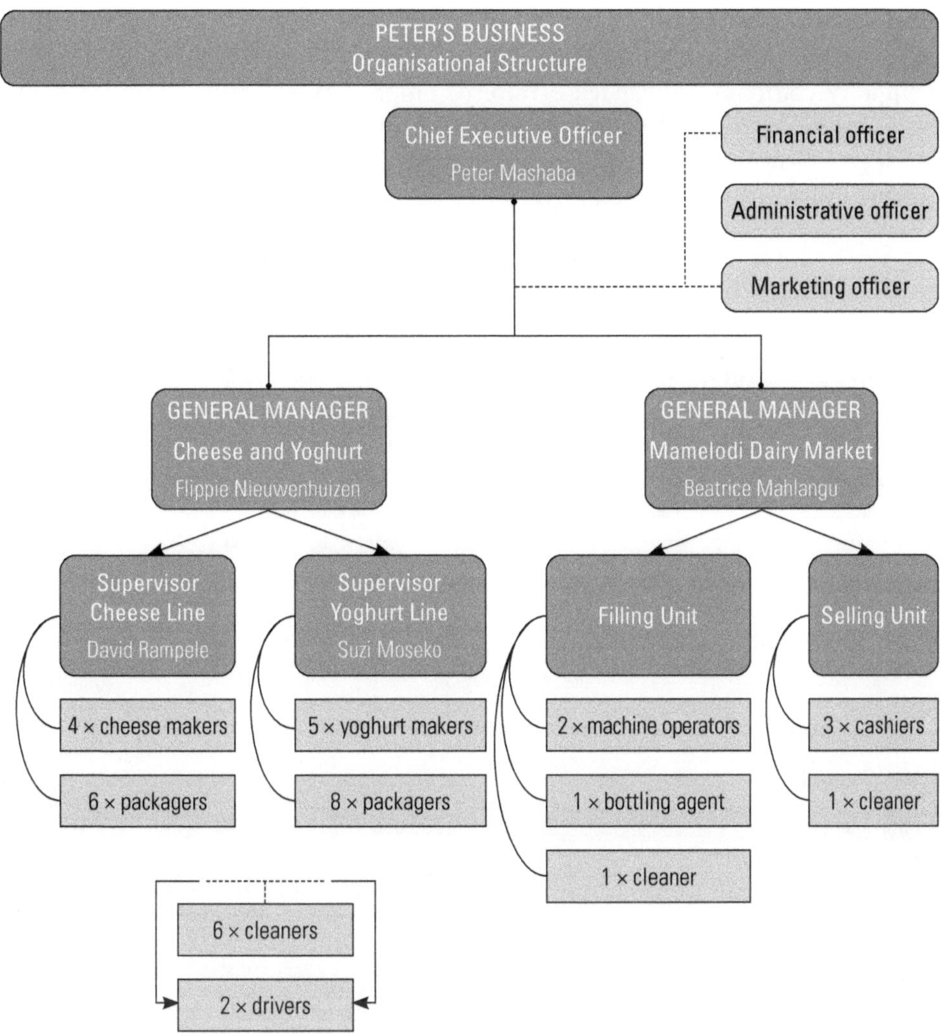

5.2 Human resources plan

Peter has formulated job descriptions and specifications for each appointment in the organisational structure. Staff will be trained in different fields.

Peter's Business complies with the following legislation:

- Labour Relations Act 66 of 1995
- Basic Conditions of Employment Act 75 of 1997
- Employment Equity Act 55 of 1998
- Skills Development Act 97 of 1998
- Skills Development Levies Act 9 of 1999.

Ownership structure

Peter is the sole member in Peter's Business (Pty) Ltd (2007/446665/23). The company complies with black economic empowerment (BEE) requirements. Peter intends to sell a 20% holding in the business in order to finance growth strategies. Another 6% will be distributed to staff members in terms of a forthcoming incentive scheme.

6. Financial plan

The financial statements in this section – the projected Statement of Financial Position, Statement of Comprehensive Income, Cash-flow Forecast and the Break-even Forecast – are merely samples that have been included for illustrative purposes only.

PETER'S BUSINESS		
PROJECTED STATEMENT OF FINANCIAL POSITION		
	REALISTIC LOCAL SCENARIO PROJECTIONS	
	2023	2024	2025
Capital employed			
Member equity			
Retained earnings	200 000	200 000	200 000
Member shareholding	500 000	500 000	500 000
	700 000	700 000	700 000
Loan	425 747	340 405	242 317
	1 125 747	1 040 405	942 317
Employment of capital			
TOTAL ASSETS	1 535 956	1 692 297	1 615 124
FIXED ASSETS	881 063	881 063	881 063
Buildings, furniture and equipment	804 738	804 738	804 738
Set-up cost	76 325	76 325	76 325

CURRENT ASSETS	654 893	811 234	734 061
Initial operating capital	81 937	81 937	81 937
Bank	572 956	729 297	652 124
Minus:			
CURRENT LIABILITIES			
Dividends payable	302 525	536 852	567 079
Receiver of Revenue	107 684	115 040	121 517
	410 209	651 892	688 596
	1 125 747	1 040 405	926 528

PETER'S BUSINESS	REALISTIC SCENARIO PROJECTIONS

STATEMENT OF COMPREHENSIVE INCOME

	PROJECTIONS			
	2023	2024	2025	Total
INCOME:	3 400 000	3 604 000	3 892 320	10 896 320
Cost of sales	1 326 000	1 405 560	1 518 005	4 249 565
Gross profit	2 074 000	2 198 440	2 374 315	6 646 755
Gross profit %	61%	61%	61%	61%
Operations expenditure	1 290 752	1 377 243	1 522 682	4 190 677
Advertising and promotions	68 000	72 080	77 846	217 926
Bank services charges	7 820	8 289	8 952	25 062
Credit card charges	38 760	41 086	44 372	124 218
Cleaning materials	5 100	5 406	5 838	16 344
First aid	1 020	1 081	1 168	3 269
Insurance	10 200	10 812	11 677	32 689
Insurance vehicles	0	0	0	0
Laundry	2 040	2 162	2 335	6 538

	2023	2024	2025	Total
Licences and permits	3 740	3 964	4 282	11 986
Medical aid	0	0	0	0
Motor expense				0
Petrol	1 000	0	24 000	25 000
Motor expense – other	0	0	5 702	5 702
Postage and delivery	340	360	389	1 090
Printing and reproduction	1 700	1 802	1 946	5 448
Professional fees				0
Accounting	7 820	8 289	8 952	25 062
Consulting	3 400	3 604	3 892	10 896
Protective clothing	4 760	5 046	5 449	15 255
Refreshments	0	0	0	0
Refuse removal	3 400	3 604	3 892	10 896
Rent (fixed)	252 632	277 895	305 684	836 211
Repairs				0
Building repairs	3 060	3 244	3 503	9 807
Computer repairs	1 020	1081	1 168	3 269
Equipment repairs	11 560	12 254	13 234	37 047
Rates and taxes	3 060	3 244	3 503	9 807
Security	4 080	4 325	4 671	13 076
Stationery and printing	3 740	3 964	4 282	11 986
Subscriptions	680	721	778	2 179
Telephone				0
Fax	1 700	1 802	1 946	5 448
Mobile	0	0	0	0
Telephone – other	3 400	3 604	3 892	10 896
Replacement of machinery	17 000	18 020	19 462	54 482
Travel and entertainment				0
Entertainment	0	0	0	0
Travel	0	0	0	0
Travel and entertainment – other	0	0	0	0
Utilities				0
Water	5 100	5 406	5 838	16 344
Gas and electric	28 220	29 913	32 306	90 439
Uniforms	3 740	3 964	4 282	11 986
Unemployment Insurance Fund	3 400	3 604	3 892	10 896
Workmen's Compensation Fund	2 380	2 523	2 725	7 627
Instalment vehicle	66 081	70 046	75 649	211 776
Gifts and donations	3 400	3 604	3 892	10 896
Member salary – A	51 000	54 060	58 385	163 445
Member salary – B	51 000	54 060	58 385	163 445
RSC levy	6 800	7 208	7 785	21 793
Salaries	258 400	273 904	295 816	828 120
Wages	336 600	356 796	385 340	1 078 736
Staff meals	10 200	10 812	11 677	32 689
Skills development	3 400	3 604	3 892	10 896
Total operating expenditure	1 290 752	1 377 243	1 522 682	4 190 677

	2023	2024	2025	Total
Net profit before financial-exp	783 248	821 197	851 633	2 456 078
Net profit BIT %	23%	23%	22%	23%
Interest expense	65 355	54 266	41 520	
Net profit before tax	717 893	766 931	810 113	2 294 937
Net profit %	21%	21%	21%	21%
Tax @ 30 %	215 368	230 079	243 034	688 481
Net profit after tax	**502 525**	**536 852**	**567 079**	**1 606 456**
%	15%	15%	15%	14,74%
Acc profit (loss) at start period	0	200 000	200 000	
Dividends paid	302 525	536 852	567 079	1 406 456
Acc profit (loss) at end of period	200 000	200 000	200 000	200 000

Index

Page numbers in italics indicate tables or figures.